AIRMONT SHAKESPEARE CLASSICS SERIES

King Henry The Fifth

By

William Shakespeare

General Introduction by Dr. David G. Pitt

AIRMONT PUBLISHING COMPANY, INC.
22 EAST 60TH STREET · NEW YORK 10022

PUBLISHED SIMULTANEOUSLY IN THE DOMINION OF CANADA
BY THE RYERSON PRESS, TORONTO

PRINTED IN THE UNITED STATES OF AMERICA
BY THE COLONIAL PRESS INC., CLINTON, MASSACHUSETTS

GENERAL INTRODUCTION

William Shakespeare: His Life, Times, and Theatre

HIS LIFE

The world's greatest poet and playwright, often called the greatest Englishman, was born in Stratford-upon-Avon, Warwickshire, in the year 1564. The exact date of his birth is uncertain, but an entry in the *Stratford Parish Register* gives his baptismal date as April 26. Since children were usually baptized two or three days after birth, it is reasonable to assume that he was born on or about April 23—an appropriate day, being the feast of St. George, the patron saint of England.

His father, John Shakespeare, was a glover and dealer in wool and farm products, who had moved to Stratford from Snitterfield, four miles distant, some time before 1552. During his early years in Stratford his business prospered, enabling him to acquire substantial property, including several houses, and to take his place among the more considerable citizens of the town. In 1557 he married Mary, daughter of Robert Arden, a wealthy landowner of Wilmcote, not far from Stratford. Two daughters were born to them before William's birth—Joan, baptized in 1558, and Margaret, baptized in 1562—but both died in infancy. William was thus their third child, though the eldest of those who survived infancy. After him were born Gilbert (1566), another Joan (1569), Anne (1571), Richard (1574), and Edmund (1580).

Very little is positively known (though much is conjectured) about Shakespeare's boyhood and education. We know that for some years after William's birth his

father's rise in Stratford society and municipal affairs
continued. Many local offices came to him in rapid succession: ale-taster, burgess (a kind of constable), assessor
of fines, chamberlain (town treasurer), high bailiff (a
kind of magistrate), alderman (town councilor), and
chief alderman in 1571. As the son of a man of such
eminence in Stratford, Shakespeare undoubtedly attended
the local Grammar School. This he was entitled to do
free of charge, his father being a town councilor. No
records of the school are extant, so that we do not know
how good a pupil he was, nor what subjects he studied. It
is probable that he covered the usual Elizabethan curricu-
lum: an "A B C book," the catechism in Latin and English, Latin grammar, the translation of Latin authors, and
perhaps some Greek grammar and translation as well. But
family circumstances appear to have curtailed his formal
education before it was complete, for shortly before William reached his fourteenth birthday his father's rising
fortunes abruptly passed their zenith.

Although we do not know all the facts, it is apparent
that about the year 1578, having gone heavily into debt,
John Shakespeare lost two large farms inherited by his
wife from her father. Thereafter, he was involved in a
series of lawsuits, and lost his post on the Stratford town
council. Matters got steadily worse for him, until finally in
1586 he was declared a bankrupt. But by this time the
future poet-dramatist was already a family man himself.

In 1582, in the midst of his father's legal and financial
crises—and perhaps because of them—Shakespeare married Anne, daughter of Richard Hathaway (recently de-
ceased) of the village of Shottery near Stratford. The
Episcopal Register for the Diocese of Worcester contains
their marriage record, dated November 28, 1582; he was
then in his eighteenth year and his wife in her twenty-
sixth. On May 26 of the following year the *Stratford
Parish Register* recorded the baptism of their first child,

Susanna; and on February 2, 1585, the baptism of a twin son and daughter named Hamnet and Judith.

These facts are all that are known of Shakespeare's early life. How he supported his family, whether he took up some trade or profession, how long he continued to live in Stratford, we do not know for certain. Tradition and conjecture have bestowed on him many interim occupations between his marriage and his appearance in London in the early fifteen-nineties: printer, dyer, traveling-player, butcher, soldier, apothecary, thief—it reads like a children's augury-rhyme (when buttons or cherry-stones are read to learn one's fate). Perhaps only the last-named "pursuit" requires some explanation. According to several accounts, one of them appearing in the first *Life* of Shakespeare by Nicholas Rowe (1709), Shakespeare fell into bad company sometime after his marriage, and on several occasions stole deer from the park of Sir Thomas Lucy, a substantial gentleman of Charlecote, near Stratford. According to Rowe:

> For this he was prosecuted by that gentleman, as he thought somewhat too severely; and in order to revenge that ill-usage, he made a ballad upon him . . . and was obliged to leave his business and family in Warwickshire, for some time, and shelter himself in London.

The story has been repeated in varying forms by most subsequent biographers, but its authenticity is doubted by many who repeat it.

Another much more attractive story, which, however, if true, does not necessarily deny the authenticity of Rowe's, is that Shakespeare during the so-called "lost years" was a schoolmaster. This, indeed, appears to be somewhat better substantiated. John Aubrey, seventeenth-century biographer and antiquary, in his *Brief Lives* (1681) declares that he had learned from a theatrical manager, whose father had known Shakespeare, that the dramatist "had been in his younger years a schoolmaster in the country." This may, then, account, in part at least, for the years between his marriage and his arrival in London about the year 1591. It is interesting to note that in two of his early plays Shakespeare includes a schoolmaster among his characters: Holofernes of *Love's Labour's Lost* and Pinch of *The Comedy of Errors*. But let us hope that neither is intended to be Shakespeare's portrait of himself!

However he may have occupied himself in the interim, we know that by 1592 he was already a budding actor and playwright in London. In that year Robert Greene in his autobiographical pamphlet *A Groatsworth of Wit*, referring to the young actors and menders of old plays who were, it seemed to him, gaining undeserved glory from the labours of their betters (both by acting their plays and by rewriting them), wrote as follows:

> Yes trust them not: for there is an upstart Crow, beautified with our feathers, that with his Tygers heart wrapt in a Players hyde, supposes he is as well able to bombast out blanke verse as the best of you: and being an absolute *Johannes factotum*, is in his owne conceit the onely Shake-scene in a countrey.

"Shakescene" is clearly Shakespeare. The phrase "upstart Crow" probably refers to his country origins and his lack of university education. "Beautified with our feathers" probably means that he uses the other playwrights' words for his own aggrandisement either in plays in which he acts or in those he writes himself. "Tygers heart wrapt in a Players hyde" is a parody of a line in III *Henry VI*, one of the earliest plays ascribed to Shakespeare. And the Latin phrase *Johannes factotum*, meaning Jack-of-all-trades, suggests that he was at this time engaged in all sorts of theatrical jobs: actor, poet, playwright, and perhaps manager as well.

Greene died shortly after making this scurrilous attack

on the young upstart from Stratford, and so escaped the resentment of those he had insulted. But Henry Chettle, himself a minor dramatist, who had prepared Greene's manuscript for the printer, in his *Kind-Harts Dreame* (1592), apologized to Shakespeare for his share in the offence:

> I am as sory as if the original fault had beene my fault, because my selfe have seene his demeanor no lesse civill, than he excelent in the qualitie he professes: Besides, divers of worship have reported his uprightness of dealing, which argues honesty, and his facetious grace in writing, that approoves his Art.

Thus, in very indirect manner and because of an attack upon him by an irascible dying man, we learn that Shakespeare at this time was in fact held in high regard by "divers of worship," that is, by many of high birth, as an upright, honest young man of pleasant manners and manifest skill as actor, poet, and playwright.

Although Shakespeare by 1593 had written, or written parts of, some five or six plays (I, II, and III *Henry VI*, *Richard III*, *The Comedy of Errors*, and perhaps *Titus Andronicus*), it was as a non-dramatic poet that he first appeared in print. *Venus and Adonis* and *The Rape of Lucrece*, long narrative poems, both bearing Shakespeare's name, were published in 1593 and 1594 respectively. But thereafter for the next twenty years he wrote almost nothing but drama. In his early period, 1591 to 1596, in addition to the plays named above he wrote *Love's Labour's Lost*, *The Taming of the Shrew*, *Two Gentlemen of Verona*, *Romeo and Juliet*, *A Midsummer Night's Dream*, *Richard II*, and *King John*. Then followed his great middle period, 1596 to 1600, during which he wrote both comedies and history-plays: *The Merchant of Venice*, I and II *Henry IV*, *The Merry Wives of Windsor*, *Much Ado about Nothing*, *Henry V*, *Julius Caesar*, *As You Like It*, and *Twelfth Night*. The period of his great

tragedies and the so-called "dark comedies" followed
(1600-1608): *Hamlet, Troilus and Cressida, All's Well
that Ends Well, Measure for Measure, Othello, King
Lear, Macbeth, Antony and Cleopatra, Timon of Athens,*
and *Coriolanus.* The last phase of his career as dramatist,
1608 to 1613, sometimes called "the period of the ro-
mances," produced *Pericles, Prince of Tyre, Cymbeline,
The Winter's Tale, The Tempest,* parts of *Henry VIII,*
and perhaps parts of *The Two Noble Kinsmen.* Many
other plays were ascribed to him, but it is doubtful that
he had a hand in any but those we have named. Long
before his death in 1616 his name held such magic for
the public that merely to print it on the title page of any
play assured its popular acclaim. The "upstart Crow" had
come a long way since 1592.

He had come a long way too from the economic straits
that may well have driven him to London many years
before. We know, for example, from the records of tax
assessments that by 1596 Shakespeare was already fairly
well-to-do. This is further borne out by his purchasing
in the following year a substantial house known as New
Place and an acre of land in Stratford for £60, a sizable
sum in those days. In 1602 he made a further purchase of
107 acres at Stratford for £320, and a cottage and more
land behind his estate at New Place. But his life during
this time was not quite unclouded. His only son, Hamnet,
died in 1596 at the age of eleven years, his father in
1601, and his mother in 1608. All three were buried in
Stratford. More happily he saw, in 1607, the marriage of
his daughter Susanna to Dr. John Hall, an eminent physi-
cian of Stratford, and, in the following year, the baptism
of his granddaughter, Elizabeth Hall.

Shakespeare's retirement to Stratford appears to have
been gradual, but by 1613, if not earlier, he seems to have
settled there, though he still went up to London occa-
sionally. Of the last months of his life we know little. We
do know that in February, 1616, his second daughter,

Judith, married Thomas Quiney. We know that on March 25, apparently already ill, Shakespeare revised and signed his will, among other bequests leaving to his wife his "second best bed with the furniture." A month later he was dead, dying on his fifty-second birthday, April 23, 1616. He was buried in the chancel of Holy Trinity Church, Stratford, on April 26.

HIS TIMES

Shakespeare lived during the English Renaissance, that age of transition that links the Mediaeval and the Modern world. Inheriting the rich traditions of the Middle Ages in art, learning, religion, and politics, rediscovering the great legacies of classical culture, the men of the Renaissance went on to new and magnificent achievements in every phase of human endeavour. No other period in history saw such varied and prolific development and expansion. And the reign of Elizabeth I (1558-1603), Shakespeare's age, was the High Renaissance in England.

Development and expansion—these are the watchwords of the age, and they apply to every aspect of life, thought, and activity. The universe grew in immensity as men gradually abandoned the old Ptolemaic view of a finite, earth-centered universe, accepting the enormous intellectual challenge of the illimitable cosmos of Copernicus's theory and Galileo's telescope. The earth enlarged, too, as more of its surface was discovered and charted by explorers following the lead of Columbus, Cabot, Magellan, and Vespucci. England itself expanded as explorers and colonizers, such as Frobisher, Davis, Gilbert, Raleigh, Grenville, Drake, and others, carried the English flag into many distant lands and seas; as English trade and commerce expanded with the opening of new markets and new sources of supply; as English sea power grew to protect the trading routes and fend off rivals, particularly Spain, the defeat of whose Invincible Armada in 1588 greatly advanced English national pride at home, and power and prestige abroad.

The world of ideas changed and expanded, too. The rediscovery and reinterpretation of the classics, with their broad and humane view of life, gave a new direction and impetus to secular education. During the Middle Ages theology had dominated education, but now the language, literature, and philosophy of the ancient world, the practical arts of grammar, logic, and rhetoric, and training in morals, manners, and gymnastics assumed the major roles in both school and university—in other words, an education that fitted one for life in the world here and now replaced one that looked rather to the life hereafter. Not that the spiritual culture of man was neglected. Indeed, it took on a new significance, for as life in this world acquired new meaning and value, religion assumed new functions, and new vitality to perform them, as the bond between the Creator and a new kind of creation.

It was, of course, the old creation—man and nature—but it was undergoing great changes. Some of these we have already seen, but the greatest was in man's conception of himself and his place in nature. The Mediaeval view of man was generally not an exalted one. It saw him as more or less depraved, fallen from Grace as a result of Adam's sin; and the things of this world, which was also "fallen," as of little value in terms of his salvation. Natural life was thought of mainly as a preparation for man's entry into Eternity. But Renaissance thought soon began to rehabilitate man, nature, and the things of this life. Without denying man's need for Grace and the value of the means of salvation provided by the Church, men came gradually to accept the idea that there were "goods," values, "innocent delights" to be had in the world here and now, and that God had given them for man to enjoy. Man himself was seen no longer as wholly vile and depraved, incapable even of desiring goodness, but rather as Shakespeare saw him in *Hamlet*:

What a piece of work is man! how noble in reason! how infinite in faculty! in form and moving how express and admirable! in action how like an angel! in apprehension how like a god! the beauty of the world! the paragon of animals!

And this is the conception of man that permeates Elizabethan thought and literature. It does not mean that man is incorruptible, immune to moral weakness and folly. Shakespeare has his villains, cowards, and fools. But man is none of these by nature; they are distortions of the true form of man. Nature framed him for greatness, endowed him with vast capacities for knowledge, achievement, and delight, and with aspirations that may take him to the stars. "O brave new world, That has such people in 't!"

The chief object of man's aspiring mind is now the natural world, whose "wondrous architecture," says Marlowe's Tamburlaine, our souls strive ceaselessly to comprehend, "Still climbing after knowledge infinite." Hamlet, too, speaks of "this goodly frame, the earth . . . this brave o'erhanging firmament, this majestical roof fretted with golden fire." No longer the ruins of a fallen paradise and the devil's, nature is seen as man's to possess, her beauty and wonder to be sought after and enjoyed, her energies to be controlled and used—as Bacon expressed it, "for the glory of the Creator and the relief of man's estate."

It was, indeed, a very stirring time to be alive in. New vistas were breaking upon the human mind and imagination everywhere. It was a time like spring, when promise, opportunity, challenge and growth appeared where none had been dreamed of before. Perhaps this is why there is so much poetry of springtime in the age of Shakespeare.

HIS THEATRE

There were many theatres, or playhouses, in Shakespeare's London. The first was built in 1576 by James

Burbage and was called the *Theatre*. It was built like an
arena, with a movable platform at one end, and had no
seats in the pit, but had benches in the galleries that surrounded it. It was built of wood, and cost about £200.
Other famous playhouses of Shakespeare's time, for the
most part similarly constructed, included the Curtain, the
Bull, the Rose, the Swan, the Fortune, and, most famous
of them all, the Globe. It was built in 1599 by the sons of
James Burbage, and it was here that most of Shakespeare's plays were performed. Since more is known about
the Globe than most of the others, I shall use it as the
basis of the brief account that follows of the Elizabethan
playhouse.

As its name suggests, the Globe was a circular structure
(the second Globe, built in 1614 after the first burned
down, was octagonal), and was open to the sky, somewhat like a modern football or baseball stadium, though
much smaller. It had three tiers of galleries surrounding
the central "yard" or pit, and a narrow roof over the top
gallery. But most interesting from our viewpoint was the
stage—or rather *stages*—which was very different from
that of most modern theatres. These have the familiar
"picture-frame" stage: a raised platform at one end of
the auditorium, framed by curtains and footlights, and
viewed only from the front like a picture. Shakespeare's
stage was very different.

The main stage, or *apron* as it was called, jutted well
out into the pit, and did not extend all the way across
from side to side. There was an area on either side for
patrons to sit or stand in, so that actors performing on the
apron could be viewed from three sides instead of one.
In addition there was an inner stage, a narrow rectangu-
lar recess let into the wall behind the main stage. When
not in use it could be closed by a curtain drawn across in
front; when open it could be used for interior scenes, ar-
bor scenes, tomb and anteroom scenes and the like. On
either side of this inner stage were doors through which

the main stage was entered. Besides the inner and outer stages there were no fewer than four other areas where the action of the play, or parts of it, might be performed. Immediately above the inner stage, and corresponding to it in size and shape, was another room with its front exposed. This was the upper stage, and was used for up-stairs scenes, or for storage when not otherwise in use. In front of this was a narrow railed gallery, which could be used for balcony scenes, or ones requiring the walls of a castle or the ramparts of a fortress. On either side of it and on the same level was a window-stage, so-called because it consisted of a small balcony enclosed by windows that opened on hinges. This permitted actors to stand inside and speak from the open windows to others on the main stage below. In all it was a very versatile multiple stage and gave the dramatist and producer much more freedom in staging than most modern theatres afford. It is interesting to note that some of the new theatres today have revived certain of the features of the Elizabethan stage.

Very little in the way of scenery and backdrops was used. The dramatist's words and the imagination of the audience supplied the lack of scenery. No special lighting effects were possible since plays were performed in the daylight that streamed in through the unroofed top of the three-tiered enclosure that was the playhouse. Usually a few standard stage-props were on hand: trestles and boards to form a table, benches and chairs, flagons, an altar, artificial trees, weapons, a man's severed head, and a few other items. Costumes were usually elaborate and gorgeous, though no attempt was made to reproduce the dress of the time and place portrayed in the play.

Play production in Shakespeare's time was clearly very different from that of ours, but we need have no doubts about the audience's response to what they saw and heard on stage. They came, they saw, and the dramatist conquered, for they kept coming back for more and more. And despite the opposition that the theatre encountered from Puritans and others, who thought it the instrument of Satan, the theatre in Shakespeare's time flourished as one of the supreme glories of a glorious age.

—DAVID G. PITT
*Memorial University of
Newfoundland.*

INTRODUCTION TO
Henry V

The Prologue to Act I of *Henry V* asks the audience to
imagine the background of olden times and stirring
events against which the players will perform the play.
Similarly, the student who reads *Henry V* must imagine
its presentation; it is very much a play of action, demanding a performance to communicate its total quality. However, only from a close study of the text can a student
develop an informed appreciation either of Shakespeare's
poetry or of his skill as a playwright in fusing into the
structure of a play the historical building blocks to which
he was bound and in transcending his sources by his own
inventions.

After study, the play assumes new dimensions of meaning; only then, with the realization of how Shakespeare
has drawn from and heightened history, can such a production as Olivier's classic film, *Henry V*, be enjoyed as
it deserves.

SOURCES AND DATE OF THE PLAY

Henry V is the eighth in a series of plays which Shakespeare wrote to dramatize English history of the 14th
and 15th centuries—*Henry VI* (three parts), *Richard III*,
Richard II, *Henry IV* (two parts), *Henry V*. Besides this
group, *King John* dramatizes a 13th century reign and
Henry VIII a 16th century one. Edward Hall's history,
*The Union of the Noble and Illustre Famelies of Lan-
castre and York* (1548), had been the source for much of
Raphael Holinshed's *Chronicles of England, Scotland,
and Ireland*; Shakespeare used the 1587 edition of
Holinshed very closely. In scenes such as Canterbury's
recital of Henry's claims to the French throne, or the

listing of the French dead after Agincourt, he is making a close verse paraphrase of Holinshed's lines. There are certain scenes, however, which seem to go back directly to Hall—the Constable's description of the English soldiers, for instance. And as critics have repeatedly pointed out, Shakespeare was almost certainly aided in his overall plan by Hall's conception of the sweep and drama of history, far more imaginatively unified than Holinshed's.

The date of *Henry V* can be established rather closely because of the reference in the Prologue of Act V:

> ". . . the general of our gracious empress—
> As in good time he may—from Ireland coming
> Bringing rebellion broached on his sword . . ."

The earl of Essex was in Ireland in 1599, putting down a rebellion in the name of Queen Elizabeth. By the summer, such high expectations of his success as Shakespeare voices were fading, and a few months later he had returned home in disgrace. The lines were applicable for only a short time, in the spring of the year.

SUBJECT MATTER OF THE PLAY

The London playgoer who came, in 1599, to see the first performance of *Henry V* by Shakespeare's company, the Chamberlain's Men, had already a background of fact and legend about the hero of Agincourt on which to base his expectations. The two chroniclers, Edward Hall and Raphael Holinshed, had established Henry V as a warrior-hero who, after a wild youth, had succeeded to the throne, "determined to put on him a new man," and had led England to glorious victory. A play called "The Famous Victories of Henry V," written by an unknown playwright and acted by the Queen's Men, probably in 1594, had shown Prince Hal in a robbery, a riot, and a courthouse scene with the wild companions of his youth, reconciled with his dying father, and then, as King, following a line of action to which Shakespeare adhered rather closely, ending with the wooing of Princess Katharine and a reconciliation with France. As well as having some awareness of the legendary hero-king, the Elizabethan playgoer would almost certainly have seen or heard of Shakespeare's version of Prince Hal's progress to kingship in *Henry IV*, Part I, 1597, and *Henry IV*, Part II, 1598.

That same London citizen in search of entertainment might well come to *Henry V* less for the story of the King than to see the continuation of the adventures of the fat knight, Falstaff, and the band of rapscallions who had been the Prince's companions in *Henry IV*, I and whose antics had outbalanced the historical action by some six hundred lines in *Henry IV*, II. In the final scene of the latter play, Falstaff foolishly and boastfully set out to engage the King's attention and recognition as Henry V rode by in procession, newly crowned. His efforts were met with stern rejection:

"I know thee not, old man: fall to thy prayers;
How ill white hairs become a fool and jester!"
(*Henry IV, Part II*, V,)

Even so, in his Epilogue, Shakespeare had promised "to continue the story, with Sir John in it." But in neither a very poor and probably pirated version of the play first printed in 1600, nor in the Folio version of 1623, upon which present texts are based, do we find more than the hostess' reports of Falstaff's illness and death. There is, however, some evidence to suggest that the Folio text was a revised one; scholars have advanced the theory that Falstaff was, indeed, in the first version, and that he was later dropped, perhaps because Will Kempe, the comic actor who had played the part, was no longer with the company. Enormous amounts of critical energy have been expended over the decades in arguing the Falstaff question; surely the weight of assembled evidence beyond the text, if any other than a careful reading is needed, suggests that in this matter, as in so many others, Shakespeare's sense of dramatic balance was impeccable. For in *Henry V*, center stage was reserved for the King; no great fat and funny knight who brought the house down in roars of laughter by his very appearance could possibly be allowed to impinge on the role of Harry of England—King and Man.

THE CAPTAINS AND THE COMIC CHARACTERS

The two groups, Fluellen, Gower, Macmorris, and Jamy, and Pistol, Nym, Bardolph, and the Hostess are, dramatically speaking, well-balanced. Their parts interlock with one another's and with the King's: Fluellen takes on Williams' quarrel with the King, Henry encounters Pistol before Agincourt, Fluellen and Gower humiliate Pistol, forcing him to eat the Welsh leek, and again, these two captains discuss the King and Falstaff. It is from the Hostess that we hear the pathetic end of Falstaff's story: her speech telling of his death touches us and, even briefly, her companions. But it is also fitting that we should hear the story from her, Pistol's Nell Quickly, for we are meant to realize that, sad though it be, in death and in life Falstaff belongs among the clownish characters and not beside the King.

Fluellen, who is entirely Shakespeare's invention, may have been given an important part to compensate the audience for Falstaff's absence—to appease the customer for the loss of one favorite by the emergence of another. Certainly he is a success, with his "Welshness," his patriotism as intense as its accent is comic, his deadly serious "professional soldier" attitude, his quick temper and tongue, and above all, his warmly human loyalty to the King. Fluellen's nationality is a compliment to the Tudor line and his personality plays a considerable part in taking *Henry V* from the level of historical tableaux to a dramatic illusion of life onstage.

THE FRENCH SCENES

In comparison to Henry and his circle, the French nobles seem a decadent, mannered, formal, and unconvincing group. Dramatically, their presence is a foil for Henry's; on such terms, Shakespeare's treatment of them is both skillful and effective. As Henry and the English, sober and God-fearing, prepare for battle, the irresponsible Dauphin, a silly boy by comparison, chafes at delay and, with his nobles, makes foolish and ill-founded boasts. It is fitting that the French should be playing-card nobles in comparison to the English and, like cardboard figures, they fell to the English archers on the field of Agincourt.

The scenes in French between Katharine and her nurse, Alice, and then between Katharine and Henry, with Alice as occasional interpreter, are quite charmingly unique in Shakespeare. Although his foundation for them may well have come from the old play of Henry V, Shakespeare's treatment is immeasurably more delicate and appealing than that of his anonymous predecessor's; the character of the King comes to shining culmination in no small measure because of the charm of his French princess and of his wooing of her.

THE CHARACTER OF THE KING

Henry, as we first see him, is the King of his legend and of his time's understanding. To a modern reader, he is apt to seem offensively calculating and piously hypocritical as he seeks advice on his "rights" to make war on France and, having been advised by the self-interested churchmen, invokes God's help to conquer France or "break it all to pieces." Our first sympathetic engagement is likely to occur as we realize the intensely passionate nature of the King and the self-discipline with which he holds it in control as he answers the stinging tennis-ball insult of the French Dauphin.

His understanding of the responsibilities of kingship and his practical administrative skill in handling matters of detail and of crises, both actual and possible, are impressive from beginning to end; as G. B. Harrison has said, "He is, above all things, efficient." Few of us living in the twentieth century are likely to undervalue quick efficiency in a leader of nations.

The other side of the coin is his ruthlessness, even cruelty: in his cat-and-mouse game with the wretched traitors, in his decision to kill the prisoners, and in the appalling threats of his speech before Harfleur. In the first two instances, Shakespeare was giving dramatic verisimilitude to already recorded events; in the last case, if Henry was undoubtedly drawing a true picture of a medieval army with license to loot and destroy, it is also well within the calculating and clever side of his character to impose the energy of his personality and language on the French in what was a successful gamble at terrifying them into surrender.

As he moves among his troops in the night before Agincourt, Henry becomes to the modern reader no less the kingly figure, but increasingly the human one, both in his encounters with his soldiers and in his musings on Ceremony, the delusive trappings of kingship, "thou proud dream, that play'st so subtly with a king's repose." He is a man of Renaissance Europe, intensely self-aware, questioning and skeptical, but no less of a believer in God and Divine Order because of it. Above all, Henry is conscious of the heavy pressures of responsibility on the shoulders of the king and, beneath the mask of royalty, of the simple humanity which is the common base of the king and all his men. Thus King Henry becomes, briefly, "a little touch of Harry in the night," and thus, too, his speech before the battle, a "set piece" expected of a king, carries a pledge of common humanity which makes it timeless:

> "We few, we happy few, we band of brothers;
> For he to-day that sheds his blood with me
> Shall be my brother . . ." (Act IV, iii, p. 105)

These scenes are so compellingly real that the King of the following battle scenes, where Shakespeare was forced into the sequence of historical events, seems comparatively lifeless, a symbol of his function, not so vividly a man.

Finally, in Act V, the King, the man, and the lover join in Henry's wooing of Princess Katharine, and at the end, he stands blunt, honest, witty, and triumphant in his pledge to her—"England is thine, Ireland is thine, France is thine, and Henry Plantagenet is thine." He is legend become man, certainly among the most vital males of Shakespeare's creation, comprising and surpassing the energy and humor of his predecessor, Hotspur, and in his inward-looking moments, even foreshadowing his great dramatic successor, Hamlet.

THE PROLOGUES OF THE PLAY

In no other play does Shakespeare so consistently set his stage and foreshadow the action of the play by means of Chorus-Prologues. Shakespeare's stage, though many-leveled and adaptable to a great variety of action, was almost bare of settings and props as we know them. One of the great demands on the Elizabethan playwright, and one to which Shakespeare rose superbly, was the indication of time, place, and surroundings within the speeches of his characters; in this play, he chooses to set his scenes, indicate the course of action and direct the audience's response in a prologue to each act and an epilogue at the end. One must imagine an actor speaking these lines, alone on the bare stage of the Globe Theatre; to read the lines imaginatively oneself is to get the impression of a crowded and brilliantly colored medieval tapestry, with its conventionalized figures breaking into the reality of speech and movement as the action begins. Finally, the Epilogue directs the spectator-reader from the triumphant man and King of Act V, to see Henry once again in the context of the past. There is great dramatic fitness in the lines which move to the impersonal, making the King a symbol of greatness and replacing his figure in the tapestry of history:

> "Thus far, with rough and all-unable pen,
> Our bending author hath pursued the story;
> In little room confining mighty men,
> Mangling by starts the full course of their glory."
>
> (Epilogue, 1-4)

And by their benedictory tone we are reminded, not only of the brevity of Henry's life, but of the magnitude of his achievement and, by implication, of the possibility of achievement for all men who must shortly pass into history:

> "Small time, but in that small, most greatly liv'd
> This star of England."   (Epilogue, 5-6)

CLARA THOMAS
York University, 1967

SUGGESTED REFERENCE WORKS

Bradley, A. C., *Oxford Lectures on Poetry*, London, 1959.

Granville-Barker, H., *Aspects of Shakespeare*, London, Oxford, 1933.

Palmer, J., *Political Characters of Shakespeare*, London, Macmillan, 1945.

Stoll, E. E., *Poets and Playwrights*, U. of Minnesota Press, 1930.

Tillyard, E. M. W., *Shakespeare's History Plays*, London, Macmillan, 1946.

Traversi, D. A., *An Approach to Shakespeare*, New York, 1956.

Van Doren, Mark, *Shakespeare*, New York, 1941.

STUDY QUESTIONS

ACT I

1. In one paragraph, give the major dates and events in the life of Henry V.

2. Identify the following English and French characters from history: Gloucester, Bedford, Exeter, York, Salisbury, Westmoreland, Warwick, Canterbury, and Ely; King of France, Dauphin, Burgundy, Orleans, Constable, Queen Katharine.

3. Write a note on Edward Hall and Raphael Holinshed. If possible, find out which passages in Act I are taken from the Chronicles. Do you consider that Shakespeare has made them more effective by turning them into verse? Give reasons, for or against.

4. Write a prose paraphrase of Canterbury's speech on order (I, ii, pp. 16-17). See what you can find out about accepted concepts of order in the Age of Elizabeth. If you can consult E. M. W. Tillyard's *The Elizabethan World Picture*, do so.

5. Read Act I carefully, noting what is said about the king before he comes on stage, and what he says for himself after his entrance. Characterize Henry V as he is revealed to you by the end of Act I.

6. Define the words expediency, cynicism, hypocrisy, honor, valor, integrity, flattery. Where, in Act I, would you find examples illustrative of any or all of these?

7. Read over the speeches of Canterbury and Ely. How has Shakespeare made these two characters distinguishable from each other? Write a paragraph on each one, giving your impression of his character.

ACT II

1. Why is Scene i, opening with Nym and Bardolph discussing the war, an effective contrast to the picture given you in the Prologue? Give examples from the text of radical and effective contrasts.

2. Read *Henry IV*, Part II, and explain why the Hostess may think it true to say of Falstaff, "the king has kill'd his heart," and why Nym and Pistol speak as they do, p. 29.

3. Write a note describing the progress of the king's unmasking of the traitors; aside from adhering to the historical account of the treasonous plot, what attributes of Henry, the King, is Shakespeare establishing? Does your acceptance of Henry's conduct here rest on an acceptance of the historical situation primarily, or do you feel that he has acted as a true leader must in any age?

4. The cynical immorality of Pistol's group can only seem amusing if one accepts the belief that the responsibility for order and power to keep order in the realm lies with the King and the nobles. Quote the speech in which Pistol voices a precept which, obviously, the noble traitors in the preceding scene had followed to their ruin.

5. Write a paragraph describing King Henry as the French Dauphin believes him to be. Then, in another paragraph, give evidence from the text to indicate that the Dauphin is wrong.

6. Contrast the attitudes of the Dauphin and the King of France to war and to the English. What do you decide of their characters from their speeches?

7. Define irony, and find some examples of its use in Act II.

ACT III

1. William Butler Yeats has said that Henry "has the gross vices, the coarse nerves, of one who is to rule among violent people . . . He is as remorseless and undistinguished as some natural force." Do you agree? Write a note on the Henry of Act III, assembling evidence from the text to comment on the foregoing statement.

2. Make a list of Shakespeare's images of war, of death, and of awesome power, in Act III, Prologue, Scene i and Scene iii.

3. Read Act III carefully and write a short paper on the dramatic effectiveness of the placing of the various scenes. Begin by drawing a curve of the dramatic intensity of the Act. How does Shakespeare achieve both intensity, and relief and variation from the intensity?

4. Write a note on Captain Fluellen, his characteristics and the part he plays in Act III.

5. Compare the pictures given you in this Act of conditions in the English and the French camps.

6. Write a character study of the Dauphin as he has been drawn from the beginning of the play, but stress particularly his portrait in Act III.

7. Write a note on Shakespeare's use of imagery centering on the horse and the dog. Find various examples of each of these categories in Act III and try to explain their effectiveness.

8. Find the two comments on Pistol, Nym, and Bardolph in Act III. What is the purpose and effect of inserting each one in its particular place?

ACT IV

1. Historians say that the French lost between 7,000 and 10,000 men at Agincourt, and that the English lost

between 400 and 500. Investigate historical accounts and write a short essay on the battle, giving reasons for the great French losses.

2. The Prologue to Act IV speaks of "A little touch of Harry in the night." Write an essay on the King's movements in the hours before the battle. How is our understanding of Henry V extended through these scenes?

3. Look up Shakespeare's *Richard II*, and in its light explain Henry's prayer, IV, i, pp. 98-99.

4. Some critics consider *Henry V* a play less artistically successful than patriotically useful in times of national emergency. To support their views, they will dismiss the King's speeches in Act II, Scene i and Act IV, Scene iii as patriotic rhetoric, nothing more. Comment on this point of view, assessing the dramatic fitness of the speeches at these points in the play; indicate any further extension they provide to the character of the king.

5. Henry's orders to his troops to kill their prisoners are historical; trace throughout Act IV Shakespeare's dramatic preparation for and justification of the King's severity.

6. While the victory at Agincourt is the dramatic center of the play's action, the two scenes between the King and Williams constitute the dramatic core of Shakespeare's characterization of the King. Write a note on these two scenes, commenting on the foregoing statement.

7. How does Shakespeare build Act IV to give his audience an imaginative comprehension of Agincourt on various levels of its action: kings, nobles, captains, common soldiers, riffraff, and even boys?

8. The King's speech on Ceremony, Scene i, pp. 96-98, is, in fact, an essay on the responsibilities of kingship. Outline those responsibilities as Henry sees them and

then write a short essay giving your opinion as to the relevance of Shakespeare's words to leaders of nations in our own day.

ACT V

1. Write a short outline of the history of England under Henry V between the battle of Agincourt and the Treaty of Troyes.

2. Describe the actions of Gower, Fluellen, and Pistol in Scene i; what does Shakespeare wish your final impression to be for each of these men, and how does he achieve his purpose?

3. What is Shakespeare's poetic method of describing France, devastated and impoverished by war? Write a note on the Duke of Burgundy's speech, Scene ii, pp. 138-139, outlining the development of this method and commenting on its effectiveness.

4. What notions do you get of the character and person of Katharine, the French princess, from Scene ii and from the earlier introductory scene, Act III, Scene iv.

5. A further facet of Henry's character is revealed to us as he woos Princess Katharine in Scene ii. Write a note on "Henry, King, Man, and Lover" as he stands at the end of Act V.

6. Such a characterization of Henry as Shakespeare has written is called a "dramatic heightening" of his historical hero. What do you see as the reasons for an epilogue concluding the play; is it more effective than finishing the play with Henry and Katharine center stage, at the end of Act V? Give reasons for your opinions.

GENERAL QUESTIONS

1. Write an essay on the historical background of *Henry V*, beginning with the reign of Richard II. Use authoritative history texts and, if possible, consult reprints of the Chronicles of Hall and Holinshed.

2. Read *Henry IV*, Part I, *Henry IV*, Part II, and *Henry V*. *Either* write an essay on Shakespeare's development of the character of Henry to its culmination in the "ideal king" of the final play, *or* trace Shakespeare's development of the character of Henry from the beginning of *Henry V* to its triumphant ending.

3. Read Machiavelli's *The Prince* and take note of the occasion and the purpose of its writing. How does Shakespeare's Henry conform to the Prince and in what respects does he diverge from him?

4. If possible, read Castiglione's *The Courtier*, taking note of its date and the purposes of its writing. Compare either the French nobles or King Henry to Castiglione's description of the noble gentleman.

5. Read *Henry IV*, Part I, *Henry IV*, Part II, and *Henry V* to trace the course of Henry's association with Falstaff. How can you justify dramatically Falstaff's non-appearance in Act V? In terms of simple necessity and expedience, why may Shakespeare have removed him from the scene?

6. Write an essay of about 800-1000 words on Shakespeare's use of Prologues and Epilogues in *Henry V*.

7. If you consider Henry's own pattern of a king to be given in his speech to the traitors, Act II, Scene ii, p. 36, describe his adherence to his formula, citing evidence

from the text for each of the qualities he mentions. Are there any admirable qualities omitted from the list that you find in Shakespeare's Henry? Illustrate from the text.

8. Write an essay of 800-1000 words on the character of Fluellen and his role throughout the play.

9. It is commonplace to speak of the "rhetoric" of *Henry V*. First define the word "rhetoric"; then give examples from the play of speeches which you believe to be "rhetorically effective," with reasons for your choices.

KING HENRY THE FIFTH

DRAMATIS PERSONAE

KING HENRY THE FIFTH.

DUKE OF GLOSTER, \
DUKE OF BEDFORD, / *brothers to the King.*

DUKE OF EXETER, *uncle to the King.*

DUKE OF YORK, *cousin to the King.*

EARL OF SALISBURY.

EARL OF WESTMORELAND.

EARL OF WARWICK.

ARCHBISHOP OF CANTERBURY.

BISHOP OF ELY.

EARL OF CAMBRIDGE.

LORD SCROOP.

SIR THOMAS GREY.

SIR THOMAS ERPINGHAM, GOWER, FLUELLEN, MACMORRIS,
   JAMY, *officers in King Henry's army.*

JOHN BATES, ALEXANDER COURT, MICHAEL WILLIAMS, *soldiers
   in the same.*

PISTOL.

NYM.

BARDOLPH.

BOY.

A HERALD.

CHARLES THE SIXTH, *King of France.*

LOUIS, *the Dauphin.*

DUKE OF BURGUNDY.

DUKE OF ORLEANS.

DUKE OF BOURBON.

THE CONSTABLE OF FRANCE.

RAMBURES, GRANDPRÉ, *French lords.*

GOVERNOR OF HARFLEUR.

MONTJOY, *a French herald.*

AMBASSADORS *to the King of England.*

ISABEL, *Queen of France.*

KATHARINE, *daughter to Charles and Isabel.*

DRAMATIS PERSONAE *continued*

ALICE, *a lady attending on her.*
HOSTESS *of a tavern in Eastcheap (formerly Mistress Quickly, and now married to Pistol).*

LORDS, LADIES, OFFICERS, SOLDIERS, CITIZENS, MESSENGERS, *and* ATTENDANTS

CHORUS.

SCENE—*England; afterwards France.*

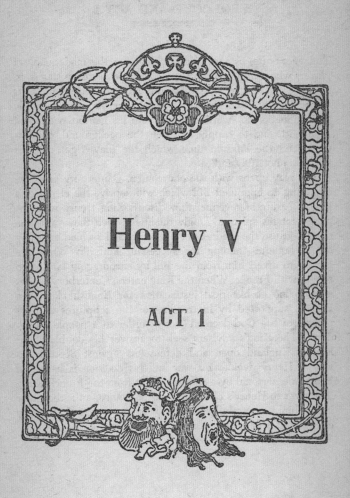

Henry V

ACT 1

PROLOGUE AND ACT I

THE PROLOGUE, ostensibly an apology for the inadequacy of players who dare to perform great, historic deeds on stages, is, in fact, a setting of the play and an announcement of its subject matter. It is also an appeal to the audience to apply its imagination to "warlike Harry" and his glorious victory at Agincourt, and to supply for itself the background, the settings, and the links in time which the playwright and his actors cannot fully indicate.

The play opens with the churchmen, Canterbury and Ely, deploring an imminent Bill which will deprive the clergy of a large measure of revenue; they discuss King Henry with approval for his splendid kingly qualities which they value the more because the wildness of his youth had seemed anything but a hopeful training for successful kingship. They are hoping to divert him from the Bill by encouraging him to go to war with France. When the King enters, Canterbury recites a long line of historical justification for English claims on France, supported by his reading of the scriptures and his picture of the God-decreed "act of order to a peopled kingdom." The King's advisers seek to answer his doubts about leaving England open and defenseless against Scottish invasion. Henry decides for war and his decision is hardened and made personal by a stinging insult from the French King; in answer to Henry's claims to land in France, an ambassador brings him a chest full of tennis balls, suggesting that Henry of England is fit only to play at trivial sport.

ACT I. Prologue.

Enter CHORUS.

CHORUS.

O for a Muse of fire,[1] that would ascend
The brightest heaven of invention,—
A kingdom for a stage, princes to act,
And monarchs to behold the swelling[2] scene!
Then should the warlike Harry, like himself,
Assume the port of Mars;[3] and at his heels,
Leasht-in like hounds, should famine, sword, and fire,
Crouch[4] for employment. But pardon, gentles[5] all,
The flat unraised[6] spirits that have dared
On this unworthy scaffold to bring forth
So great an object: can this cockpit[7] hold
The vasty[8] fields of France? or may we cram
Within this wooden O[9] the very casques[10]
That did affright the air at Agincourt?
O, pardon! since a crooked figure may
Attest in little place a million;
And let us, ciphers to this great accompt,[11]
On your imaginary forces work.
Suppose within the girdle of these walls
Are now confined two mighty monarchies,
Whose high-upreared and abutting fronts[12]
The perilous narrow ocean[13] parts asunder:
Piece-out our imperfections with your thoughts;
Into a thousand parts divide one man,
And make imaginary puissance;[14]

---

[1] fire: burning inspiration. [2] swelling: stirring; majestic. [3] the port of Mars: the bearing and appearance of the god of war. [4] Crouch: be ready to spring. [5] gentles: gentlefolk; gentle spectators. [6] flat unraised: uninspired. [7] cockpit: i.e., playhouse; pit of a theatre. [8] vasty: vast; trackless. [9] wooden O: the circular stage of the Globe Theatre. [10] casques: war helmets. [11] accompt: account. [12] fronts: the cliffs of Calais and Dover. [13] perilous narrow ocean: the English Channel. [14] puissance: strength.

Think, when we talk of horses, that you see them
Printing their proud hoofs i'th'receiving earth;—
For 'tis your thoughts that now must deck our kings,
Carry them here and there; jumping o'er times,
Turning th'accomplishment of many years
Into an hour-glass;[1] for the which supply,
Admit me Chorus to this history;
Who, prologue-like, your humble patience pray,
Gently to hear, kindly to judge, our play.   [*Exit.*

---

[1] Turning th'accomplishment . . . hour-glass: telescoping the happenings of years into a few hours' time.

ACT I. Scene I.

London. An ante-chamber in the KING'S *palace.*

Enter the ARCHBISHOP OF CANTERBURY *and the* BISHOP OF ELY.

ARCHBISHOP OF CANTERBURY.

My lord, I'll tell you,—that self[1] bill is urged,
Which in th'eleventh year of the last king's reign[2]
Was like,[3] and had indeed against us past,
But that the scambling[4] and unquiet time
Did push it out of further question.[5]

BISHOP OF ELY.

But how, my lord, shall we resist it now?

ARCHBISHOP OF CANTERBURY.

It must be thought on. If it pass against us,
We lose the better half of our possession;
For all the temporal lands,[6] which men devout
By testament have given to the church,
Would they strip from us; being valued thus,—
As much as would maintain, to the king's honour,
Full fifteen earls and fifteen hundred knights,
Six thousand and two hundred good esquires;
And, to relief of lazars[7] and weak age,
Of indigent faint souls past corporal[8] toil,
A hundred almshouses right well supplied;
And to the coffers of the king, beside,[9]
A thousand pounds by th'year: thus runs the bill.

BISHOP OF ELY.

This would drink deep.

---

[1] self: selfsame.   [2] last king's reign: i.e., Henry IV's reign.   [3] Was
like: was likely to come to pass.   [4] scambling: disordered.
[5] question: consideration.   [6] temporal lands: estates not belonging
to the church.   [7] lazars: lepers; beggars.   [8] corporal: corporeal;
bodily; physical.   [9] beside: besides.

ARCHBISHOP OF CANTERBURY.

　　　　　　　　　　'Twould drink the cup and all.

BISHOP OF ELY.

But what prevention? [1]

ARCHBISHOP OF CANTERBURY.

The king is full of grace and fair regard.

BISHOP OF ELY.

And a true lover of the holy church.

ARCHBISHOP OF CANTERBURY.

The courses of his youth promised it not.
The breath no sooner left his father's body,
But that his wildness, mortified[2] in him,
Seem'd to die too; yea, at that very moment,
Consideration,[3] like an angel, came,
And whipt th'offending Adam[4] out of him,
Leaving his body as a paradise,
T'envelop and contain celestial spirits.
Never was such a sudden scholar made;
Never came reformation in a flood,
With such a heady current,[5] scouring[6] faults;
Nor never Hydra-headed[7] wilfulness
So soon did lose his seat, and all at once,
As in this king.

BISHOP OF ELY.

　　　　　　　We are blessed in the change.

ARCHBISHOP OF CANTERBURY.

Hear him but reason in divinity,[8]
And, all-admiring, with an inward wish
You would desire the king were made a prelate:
Hear him debate of commonwealth affairs,
You would say it hath been all-in-all his study:[9]
List[10] this discourse of war, and you shall hear
A fearful battle render'd you in music:

---

[1] what prevention: what must be done to prevent this.　[2] mortified: killed.　[3] Consideration: thoughtfulness.　[4] Adam: a symbol of original human sin.　[5] heady current: tumultuous flood.　[6] scouring: cleansing.　[7] Hydra-headed: an allusion to the many-headed sea monster of Greek mythology killed by Hercules.　[8] divinity: theology.　[9] all-in-all his study: i.e., his only study.　[10] List: listen to.

Turn him to any cause of policy,[1]
The Gordian knot[2] of it he will unloose,
Familiar as his garter:—that, when he speaks,
The air, a charter'd libertine,[3] is still,
And the mute wonder lurketh in men's ears,
To steal his sweet and honey'd sentences;
So that the art and practic part[4] of life
Must be the mistress to[5] this theoric:
Which is a wonder how his Grace should glean it,
Since his addiction was to courses vain;
His companies[6] unletter'd, rude, and shallow;
His hours fill'd up with riots, banquets, sports;
And never noted in him any study,
Any retirement, any sequestration[7]
From open haunts[8] and popularity.[9]

BISHOP OF ELY.

The strawberry grows underneath the nettle,
And wholesome berries thrive and ripen best
Neighbour'd by fruit of baser quality:
And so the prince obscured his contemplation
Under the veil of wildness; which, no doubt,
Grew like the summer grass, fastest by night,
Unseen, yet crescive[10] in his faculty.

ARCHBISHOP OF CANTERBURY.

It must be so; for miracles are ceased;
And therefore we must needs admit the means[11]
How things are perfected.

BISHOP OF ELY.

                    But, my good lord,
How now for mitigation of this bill
Urged by the commons? Doth his majesty
Incline to it, or no?

---

[1] cause of policy: problem of state.   [2] Gordian knot: he who un-
tied the knot of Gordius, King of Phrygia, would become ruler of
Asia; Alexander the Great, failing to untie it, cut the knot.   [3] a
charter'd libertine: free (licensed) to go where it wishes.   [4] art
and practic part: training and practical experience.   [5] the mistress
to: superior to.   [6] companies: companions.   [7] sequestration:
withdrawal.   [8] open haunts: public places.   [9] popularity: vul-
garity.   [10] crescive: increasing.   [11] admit the means: accept the
natural cause.

ARCHBISHOP OF CANTERBURY.

He seems indifferent;[1]
Or, rather, swaying more upon our part[2]
Than cherishing[3] th'exhibiters[4] against us:
For I have made an offer to his majesty,—
Upon[5] our spiritual convocation,[6]
And in regard of causes now in hand,
Which I have open'd[7] to his Grace at large,[8]
As touching France,—to give a greater sum
Than ever at one time the clergy yet
Did to his predecessors part withal.

BISHOP OF ELY.

How did this offer seem received, my lord?

ARCHBISHOP OF CANTERBURY.

With good acceptance of his majesty;
Save that there was not time enough to hear—
As, I perceived, his Grace would fain have done—
The severals and unhidden passages[9]
Of his true titles to some certain dukedoms,
And, generally, to the crown and seat of France,
Derived from Edward,[10] his great-grandfather.

BISHOP OF ELY.

What was th'impediment that broke this off?

ARCHBISHOP OF CANTERBURY.

The French ambassador upon that instant
Craved audience;—and the hour, I think, is come
To give him hearing: is it four o'clock?

BISHOP OF ELY.

It is.

ARCHBISHOP OF CANTERBURY.

Then go we in, to know his embassy;[11]
Which I could, with a ready guess, declare,
Before the Frenchman speak a word of it.

---

[1] indifferent: impartial. [2] swaying more upon our part: "inclining our way"—Rolfe. [3] cherishing: favoring. [4] th'exhibiters: the introducers or supporters of the bill in parliament. [5] Upon: in accordance with. [6] spiritual convocation: a meeting of the religious heads. [7] open'd: revealed, or explained. [8] at large: fully. [9] severals . . . passages: the details and clear lines of succession. [10] Edward: Edward III. [11] embassy: mission.

BISHOP OF ELY.

I'll wait upon you; and I long to hear it.   [*Exeunt.*

SCENE II.

The same. The Presence-chamber.

Enter KING HENRY, GLOSTER, BEDFORD, EXETER, WARWICK, WESTMORELAND, *and* ATTENDANTS.

KING HENRY.

Where is my gracious Lord of Canterbury?

DUKE OF EXETER.

Not here in presence.

KING HENRY.

                    Send for him, good uncle.[1]

EARL OF WESTMORELAND.

Shall we call in th'ambassador, my liege?

KING HENRY.

Not yet, my cousin: we would be resolved,[2]
Before we hear him, of some things of weight,
That task[3] our thoughts, concerning us and France.

Enter the ARCHBISHOP OF CANTERBURY *and the* BISHOP OF ELY.

ARCHBISHOP OF CANTERBURY.

God and his angels guard your sacred throne,
And make you long become it!

KING HENRY.

                    Sure, we thank you.

My learned lord, we pray you to proceed,
And justly and religiously unfold
Why the law Salique,[4] that they have in France,
Or[5] should, or should not, bar us in our claim:

---

[1] good uncle: the Earl of Dorset, half-brother of Henry IV, was made Duke of Exeter after the Battle of Agincourt.   [2] be resolved: be satisfied.   [3] task: occupy.   [4] the law Salique: the Salic law of the Franks, from which derived the custom that a woman could not inherit the throne of France.   [5] Or: either.

And God forbid, my dear and faithful lord,
That you should fashion, wrest, or bow your reading,
Or nicely charge your understanding soul
With opening titles miscreate,[1] whose right
Suits not[2] in native colours with the truth;
For God doth know how many, now in health,
Shall drop their blood in approbation[3]
Of what your reverence shall incite us to.
Therefore take heed how you impawn[4] our person,
How you awake the sleeping sword of war:
We charge you, in the name of God, take heed;
For never two such kingdoms did contend
Without much fall of blood;[5] whose guiltless drops
Are every one a woe, a sore complaint
'Gainst him whose wrongs give edge unto the swords
That make such waste in brief mortality.[6]
Under this conjuration, speak, my lord;
For we will hear, note, and believe in heart
That what you speak is in your conscience washt
As pure as sin with baptism.

ARCHBISHOP OF CANTERBURY.

Then hear me, gracious sovereign,—and you peers,
That owe yourselves, your lives, and services
To this imperial throne.—There is no bar
To make against your highness' claim to France
But this, which they produce from Pharamond,—
In terram Salican mulieres ne succedant,
'No woman shall succeed in Salique land:'
Which Salique land the French unjustly gloze[7]
To be the realm of France, and Pharamond

---

[1] nicely charge . . . miscreate: knowing that it is not the truth, burden yourself with hopes based on false claims. [2] Suits not: does not match. [3] in approbation: in proving. [4] impawn: pledge. [5] fall of blood: bloodshed. [6] in brief mortality: of young lives. [7] gloze: pretend; freely interpret.

The founder of this law and female bar.
Yet their own authors faithfully affirm
That the land Salique is in Germany,
Between the floods[1] of Sala and of Elbe;
Where Charles the Great,[2] having subdued the Saxons,
There left behind and settled certain French;
Who, holding in disdain the German women
For some dishonest manners[3] of their life,
Establisht then this law,—to wit, no female
Should be inheritrix in Salique land:
Which Salique, as I said, 'twixt Elbe and Sala,
Is at this day in Germany call'd Meisen.[4]
Then doth it well appear, the Salique law
Was not devised for the realm of France:
Nor did the French possess the Salique land
Until four hundred one and twenty years
After defunction[5] of King Pharamond,
Idly[6] supposed the founder of this law;
Who died within the year of our redemption
Four hundred twenty-six; and Charles the Great
Subdued the Saxons, and did seat the French
Beyond the river Sala, in the year
Eight hundred five. Besides, their writers say,
King Pepin, which deposed Childeric,
Did, as heir general, being descended
Of Blithild, which was daughter to King Clothair,
Make claim and title to the crown of France.
Hugh Capet also,—who usurpt the crown
Of Charles the duke of Lorraine, sole heir male
Of the true line and stock of Charles the Great,—
To find his title with some shows of truth,
Though, in pure truth, it was corrupt and naught,

---

[1] floods: waters.
[2] Charles the Great: Charlemagne.
[3] dishonest manners: immoral conduct.
[4] Meisen: Meissen.
[5] defunction: the death.
[6] Idly: foolishly.

Convey'd himself[1] as heir to th'Lady Lingare,
Daughter to Charlemain, who was the son
To Louis the emperor, and Louis the son
Of Charles the Great. Also King Louis the Tenth,
Who was sole heir to the usurper Capet,
Could not keep quiet in his conscience,
Wearing the crown of France, till satisfied
That fair Queen Isabel, his grandmother,
Was lineal of[2] the Lady Ermengare,[3]
Daughter to Charles the foresaid duke of Lorraine:
By the which marriage the line of Charles the Great
Was re-united to the crown of France.
So that, as clear as is the summer's sun,
King Pepin's title, and Hugh Capet's claim,
King Louis his satisfaction,[4] all appear
To hold in right and title of the female:
So do the kings of France unto this day;
Howbeit they would hold up this Salique law
To bar your highness claiming from the female;
And rather choose to hide them in a net[5]
Than amply to imbar[6] their crooked titles
Usurpt from you and your progenitors.

KING HENRY.

May I with right and conscience make this claim?

ARCHBISHOP OF CANTERBURY.

The sin upon my head, dread sovereign!
For in the Book of Numbers[7] is it writ,—
When the man dies,[8] let the inheritance
Descend unto the daughter. Gracious lord,

---

[1] Convey'd himself: put forth his claim.   [2] lineal of: directly descended from.   [3] Ermengare: Ermengard, according to Holinshed.   [4] King Louis his satisfaction: that is, to King Louis' satisfaction.   [5] net: intricate but open deception.   [6] imbar: secure. [7] the Book of Numbers: see Numbers 27:8.   [8] When the man dies: that is, when the king dies without a son as successor.

Stand for your own; unwind your bloody flag;
Look back into your mighty ancestors:
Go, my dread Lord, to your great-grandsire's[1] tomb,
From whom you claim; invoke his warlike spirit,
And your great-uncle's, Edward the Black Prince,
Who on the French ground play'd a tragedy,[2]
Making defeat on the full power of France,
Whiles[3] his most mighty father on a hill
Stood smiling to behold his lion's whelp
Forage[4] in blood of French nobility.
O noble English, that could entertain
With half their forces the full pride of France,
And let another half stand laughing by,
All out of work and cold for action![5]

BISHOP OF ELY.

Awake remembrance of these valiant dead,
And with your puissant[6] arm renew their feats:
You are their heir; you sit upon their throne;
The blood and courage that renowned them
Runs in your veins; and my thrice-puissant[7] liege
Is in the very May-morn of his youth,
Ripe for exploits and mighty enterprises.

DUKE OF EXETER.

Your brother kings and monarchs of the earth
Do all expect that you should rouse yourself,
As did the former lions of your blood.

EARL OF WESTMORELAND.

They know your Grace hath cause and means and might;
So hath your highness; never king of England
Had nobles richer and more loyal subjects,

---

[1] great-grandsire: Edward III.   [2] a tragedy: the Battle of Crécy (1346).   [3] Whiles: while.   [4] Forage: ravaging; seeking his prey. [5] cold for action: "cold for lack of action"—Malone.   [6] puissant: mighty.   [7] thrice-puissant: that is, mighty in his own right and preceded by two mighty ancestors.

Whose hearts have left their bodies here in England,
And lie pavilion'd[1] in the fields of France.

ARCHBISHOP OF CANTERBURY.

O, let their bodies follow, my dear liege,
With blood and sword and fire to win your right:
In aid whereof we of the spirituality[2]
Will raise your highness such a mighty sum
As never did the clergy at one time
Bring in to any of your ancestors.

KING HENRY.

We must not only arm t'invade the French,
But lay down our proportions[3] to defend
Against the Scot, who will make road upon[4] us
With all advantages.[5]

ARCHBISHOP OF CANTERBURY.

They of those marches,[6] gracious sovereign,
Shall be a wall sufficient to defend
Our inland from the pilfering borderers.[7]

KING HENRY.

We do not mean the coursing snatchers only,
But fear the main intendment[8] of the Scot,
Who hath been still a giddy[9] neighbour to us;
For you shall read that my great-grandfather
Never went with his forces into France,
But that the Scot on his unfurnisht[10] kingdom
Came pouring, like the tide into a breach,
With ample and brim fullness of his force;
Galling the gleaned[11] land with hot assays,[12]
Girding with grievous siege castles and towns;
That England, being empty of defence,
Hath shook and trembled at th'ill neighbourhood.

---

[1] pavilion'd: in their tents.   [2] spirituality: clergy.   [3] lay down our proportions: allocate the proper number of troops.   [4] make road upon: raid; invade.   [5] With all advantages: with everything in their favor.   [6] marches: borders.   [7] pilfering borderers: unorganized border raiders.   [8] intendment: intentions; plans.   [9] giddy: unstable.   [10] unfurnisht: defenseless; unprotected.   [11] gleaned: stripped (of soldiers).   [12] assays: forays.

ARCHBISHOP OF CANTERBURY.

She hath been then more fear'd[1] than harm'd, my liege;
For hear her but exampled by herself:—
When all her chivalry hath been in France,
And she a mourning widow of her nobles,
She hath herself not only well defended
But taken, and impounded[2] as a stray,
The King of Scots;[3] whom she did send to France,
To fill King Edward's fame with prisoner kings,
And make her chronicle as rich with praise
As is the ooze and bottom of the sea
With sunken wrack[4] and sumless[5] treasuries.

EARL OF WESTMORELAND.

But there's a saying, very old and true,—

'If that you will France win,
Then with Scotland first begin:'

For once the eagle England being in prey,[6]
To her unguarded nest the weasel Scot
Comes sneaking, and so sucks her princely eggs;
Playing the mouse in absence of the cat,
To spoil and havoc more than she can eat.

DUKE OF EXETER.

It follows, then, the cat must stay at home:
Yet that is but a curst necessity,
Since we have locks to safeguard necessaries,
And pretty traps to catch the petty thieves.
While that the armed hand doth fight abroad,
Th'advised[7] head defends itself at home;
For government, though high, and low, and lower,
Put into parts,[8] doth keep in one concent,[9]
Congreeing[10] in a full and natural close,[11]
Like music.

---

[1] fear'd: frightened.   [2] impounded: held in jail.   [3] King of Scots:
David II, captured at Neville's Cross (1346) while Edward III was
in France.   [4] wrack: wreck.   [5] sumless: priceless.   [6] in prey:
after prey; in search of prey.   [7] advised: prudent; thoughtful.
[8] Put into parts: divided among the various heads of state, as are
the various parts of music among the players.   [9] concent: consent;
harmony.   [10] Congreeing: harmonizing.   [11] close: cadence.

ARCHBISHOP OF CANTERBURY.

     True: therefore doth heaven divide
The state of man in divers functions,
Setting endeavour in continual motion;[1]
To which is fixed, as an aim or butt,[2]
Obedience: for so work the honey-bees,
Creatures that, by a rule in nature, teach
The art of order to a peopled kingdom.
They have a king, and officers of sorts:
Where some, like magistrates, correct[3] at home;
Others, like merchants, venture trade abroad;
Others, like soldiers, armed in their stings,
Make boot upon[4] the summer's velvet buds;
Which pillage they with merry march bring home
To the tent-royal of their emperor:
Who, busied in his majesty,[5] surveys
The singing masons building roofs of gold;
The civil[6] citizens kneading-up the honey;
The poor mechanic porters crowding in
Their heavy burdens at his narrow gate;
The sad-eyed[7] justice, with his surly hum,
Delivering o'er to executors[8] pale
The lazy yawning drone. I this infer,—
That many things, having full reference
To one concent,[9] may work contrariously:
As many arrows, loosed several ways,[10]
Fly to one mark;
As many several ways meet in one town;
As many fresh streams run in one self[11] sea;
As many lines close in the dial's[12] centre;
So may a thousand actions, once afoot,
End in one purpose, and be all well borne

---

[1] Setting endeavour . . . motion: that is, all working for the common good. [2] butt: target. [3] correct: set things in order. [4] Make boot upon: plunder. [5] busied in his majesty: occupied with his royal responsibilities. [6] civil: well-governed. [7] sad-eyed: sober looking; grave. [8] executors: executioners. [9] To one concent: toward one aim. [10] loosed several ways: shot from separate directions. [11] self: selfsame. [12] dial's: sundial's.

Without defeat. Therefore to France, my liege.

Divide your happy England into four;

Whereof take you one quarter into France,

And you withal shall make all Gallia shake.

If we, with thrice such powers[1] left at home,

Cannot defend our own doors from the dog,

Let us be worried,[2] and our nation lose

The name of hardiness and policy.[3]

   KING HENRY.

Call in the messengers sent from the Dauphin.[4]

              [*Exeunt some* ATTENDANTS.

Now are we well resolved; and, by God's help,

And yours, the noble sinews[5] of our power,

France being ours, we'll bend it to our awe,

Or break it all to pieces: or there we'll sit,

Ruling in large and ample empery[6]

O'er France and all her almost kingly dukedoms,

Or lay these bones in an unworthy[7] urn,

Tombless, with no remembrance over them:

Either our history shall with full mouth

Speak freely of our acts, or else our grave,

Like Turkish mute, shall have a tongueless mouth,

Not worshipt with a waxen[8] epitaph.

   Enter AMBASSADORS *of France, attended.*

Now are we well prepared to know the pleasure

Of our fair cousin Dauphin; for we hear

Your greeting is from him, not from the king.

   FIRST AMBASSADOR.

May't please your majesty to give us leave

Freely to render what we have in charge;[9]

Or shall we sparingly show you far off [10]

The Dauphin's meaning and our embassy?

---

[1] powers: forces.   [2] worried: harried.   [3] policy: wisdom in affairs of state.   [4] Dauphin: the prince next in succession to the throne of France.   [5] sinews: supports.   [6] empery: dominion.
[7] unworthy: unhonored.   [8] a waxen: i.e., an easily erased.
[9] what we have in charge: what we have been entrusted to convey.
[10] sparingly . . . off: spare your feelings by hiding part of the truth.

KING HENRY.

We are no tyrant, but a Christian king;
Unto whose grace our passion is as subject
As are our wretches fetter'd in our prisons:
Therefore with frank and with uncurbed plainness
Tell us the Dauphin's mind.

FIRST AMBASSADOR.

Thus, then, in few.[1]

Your highness, lately sending into France,
Did claim some certain dukedoms, in the right
Of your great predecessor, King Edward the Third.
In answer of which claim, the prince our master
Says, that you savour too much of your youth;[2]
And bids you be advised,[3] there's naught in France
That can be with a nimble galliard[4] won;—
You cannot revel into dukedoms there.
He therefore sends you, meeter[5] for your spirit,
This tun[6] of treasure; and, in lieu of this,
Desires you let the dukedoms that you claim
Hear no more of you. This the Dauphin speaks.

KING HENRY.

What treasure, uncle?

DUKE OF EXETER.

Tennis-balls, my liege.

KING HENRY.

We are glad the Dauphin is so pleasant with us;
His present and your pains we thank you for:
When we have matcht our rackets to these balls,
We will, in France, by God's grace, play a set[7]
Shall strike his father's crown into the hazard.[8]

---

[1] in few: in a few words.   [2] you savour too much of your youth: that is, you act recklessly, without thought.   [3] advised: informed. [4] galliard: sprightly French dance.   [5] meeter: more suitable. [6] tun: keg; barrel.   [7] set: set of tennis.   [8] hazard: a difficult part of the tennis court to reach.

Tell him he hath made a match with such a wrangler[1]
That all the courts of France will be disturb'd
With chases.[2] And we understand him well,
How he comes o'er us with[3] our wilder days,
Not measuring what use we made of them.
We never valued this poor seat of England;[4]
And therefore, living hence, did give ourself
To barbarous licence; as 'tis ever common
That men are merriest when they are from home.[5]
But tell the Dauphin, I will keep my state,[6]
Be like a king, and show my sail of greatness,[7]
When I do rouse me in[8] my throne of France:
For that I have laid by my majesty,
And plodded like a man for working-days;[9]
But I will rise there with so full a glory,
That I will dazzle all the eyes of France,
Yea, strike the Dauphin blind to look on us.
And tell the pleasant prince, this mock of his
Hath turn'd his balls to gun-stones,[10] and his soul
Shall stand sore charged for the wasteful vengeance
That shall fly with them: for many a thousand widows
Shall this his mock mock out of their dear husbands;
Mock mothers from their sons, mock castles down;
And some are yet ungotten[11] and unborn
That shall have cause to curse the Dauphin's scorn.
But this lies all within the will of God,
To whom I do appeal; and in whose name,

---

[1] wrangler: opponent.   [2] chases: missed returns in tennis, with the
second meaning of *forays*.   [3] comes o'er us with: seeks to belittle
us with; reminds us of.   [4] this poor seat of England: i.e., the
throne of France.   [5] from home: away from home.   [6] state: dignity.   [7] my sail of greatness: my natural kingly grace.   [8] rouse
me in: raise myself up to.   [9] man for working-days: day laborer.
[10] gun-stones: cannon balls.   [11] ungotten: unbegotten.

Tell you the Dauphin, I am coming on,
To venge me[1] as I may, and to put forth
My rightful hand in a well-hallow'd cause.
So, get you hence in peace; and tell the Dauphin,
His jest will savour but of shallow wit,
When thousands weep, more than did laugh at it.—
Convey them with safe conduct.—Fare you well.

[*Exeunt* AMBASSADORS.

    DUKE OF EXETER.

This was a merry message.

    KING HENRY.

We hope to make the sender blush at it.
Therefore, my lords, omit no happy[2] hour
That may give furtherance to our expedition;
For we have now no thought in us but France,
Save those to God, that run before our business.[3]
Therefore let our proportions[4] for these wars
Be soon collected, and all things thought upon
That may with reasonable swiftness add
More feathers to our wings; for, God before,[5]
We'll chide this Dauphin at his father's door.
Therefore let every man now task[6] his thought,
That this fair action may on foot be brought.

[*Flourish. Exeunt.*

---

[1] To venge me: to avenge myself.   [2] happy: propitious.   [3] to
God . . . business: that is, all our endeavors are preceded by
prayers to God for guidance.   [4] proportions: allocation of troops.
[5] God before: with God leading us.   [6] task: belabor; strain.

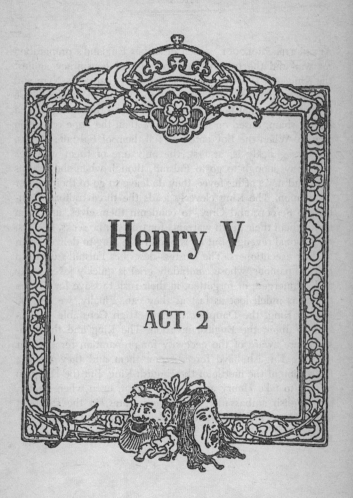

Henry V

ACT 2

ACT II

AFTER THE PROLOGUE, which describes England's preparation for war and the treacherous French-paid conspiracy against the King, Act II opens with the clownish characters Nym and Bardolph, joined shortly by Pistol and Hostess Quickly. These men are playing at being brave soldiers, and their "valour" is a hollow sham, based on nothing more than the hope of loot in France. When the Boy enters to tell them of Falstaff's illness, Mistress Quickly is, at first, the only one of them who has sympathy enough to go to Falstaff, though when she returns with bad news of his fever, they do leave to go to their former companion. The King cleverly leads the three traitors, Cambridge, Scroop, and Grey, to condemn themselves, and then hands them their death warrants for treason; he seeks, he says, no personal revenge, but he is bound as a king to deliver them to their executioners. The Hostess describes Falstaff's death to her companions, whose comradely grief is quickly joked away and submerged, or forgotten, in their rush to leave for France to get as much loot as fast as they can. Finally, we see the French King, the Dauphin, and the High Constable in conference about the English invasion. The King and the Constable are aware of the necessity for preparation for the war that the English have forced upon them and they show a realization of the mettle of the English King. But the Dauphin refuses to take Henry as a serious threat, even when Exeter, the English ambassador, enters and states, in the strongest terms, Henry's claims from and defiance of the French.

ACT II. PROLOGUE.

Enter CHORUS.

CHORUS.

Now all the youth of England are on fire,
And silken dalliance[1] in the wardrobe lies:
Now thrive the armourers, and honour's thought
Reigns solely in the breast of every man:
They sell the pasture now to buy the horse;
Following the mirror[2] of all Christian kings,

---

[1] silken dalliance: frivolous thoughts.
[2] mirror: pattern; behavior.

With winged heels, as English Mercuries.[1]
For now sits Expectation in the air,
And hides a sword from hilts unto the point
With crowns imperial, crowns, and coronets,
Promised to Harry and his followers.
The French, advised by good intelligence[2]
Of this most dreadful preparation,
Shake in their fear; and with pale policy[3]
Seek to divert the English purposes.
O England!—model to thy inward greatness,
Like little body with a mighty heart,—
What mightst thou do, that honour would thee do,[4]
Were all thy children kind and natural! [5]
But see thy fault! France hath in thee found out
A nest of hollow bosoms,[6] which he fills
With treacherous crowns;[7] and three corrupted men,—
One, Richard earl of Cambridge;[8] and the second,
Henry Lord Scroop of Masham;[9] and the third,
Sir Thomas Grey, knight, of Northumberland,—
Have, for the gilt[10] of France—O guilt indeed!—
Confirm'd conspiracy with fearful France;
And by their hands this grace of kings[11] must die,
If hell and treason hold their promises,
Ere he take ship for France, and in Southampton.
Linger[12] your patience on; and we'll digest
Th'abuse of distance;[13] force a play.
The sum is paid; the traitors are agreed;

---

[1] **English Mercuries:** an allusion to winged Mercury, messenger of the gods.   [2] **intelligence:** spies.   [3] **pale policy:** weak statecraft.   [4] **that honour would thee do:** that would be honorable for you to do.   [5] **kind and natural:** loving and filled with filial devotion.   [6] **hollow bosoms:** false hearts.   [7] **treacherous crowns:** gold paid for treachery.   [8] **Richard earl of Cambridge:** younger son of Edmund of Langley, Duke of York and cousin of Henry IV.   [9] **Henry Lord Scroop of Masham:** husband of Joan, Duchess of York.   [10] **gilt:** gold.   [11] **this grace of kings:** this king who does honor to the title.   [12] **Linger:** hold.   [13] **digest/Th'abuse of distance:** try to make palatable the difficulties of telescoping time and distance.

The king is set[1] from London; and the scene
Is now transported, gentles,[2] to Southampton,—
There is the playhouse now, there must you sit:
And thence to France shall we convey you safe,
And bring you back, charming the narrow seas[3]
To give you gentle pass;[4] for, if we may,
We'll not offend one stomach with our play.
But, till the king come forth, and not till then,
Unto Southampton do we shift our scene.   [*Exit.*

Scene I.

London. Before the Boar's Head Tavern, Eastcheap.

Enter CORPORAL NYM *and* LIEUTENANT BARDOLPH.

BARDOLPH.

Well met, Corporal Nym.

NYM.

Good morrow, Lieutenant Bardolph.

BARDOLPH.

What, are Ancient[5] Pistol and you friends yet?

NYM.

For my part, I care not: I say little; but when time shall serve,
there shall be smiles;—but that shall be as it may. I dare not
fight; but I will wink,[6] and hold out mine iron: it is a simple
one; but what though? it will toast cheese, and it will endure
cold as another man's sword will: and there's the humour of
it.[7]

BARDOLPH.

I will bestow a breakfast to make you friends; and we'll be all

---

[1] is set: has set out.   [2] gentles: gentlefolk.   [3] charming the narrow seas: making the English Channel smooth.   [4] pass: passage.
[5] Ancient: ensign; lieutenant.   [6] wink: close an eye.   [7] humour of it: that is, the ability to adapt oneself to a situation; *humour* is Nym's favorite word.

three sworn brothers[1] to France: let's be so, good Corporal Nym.

NYM.

Faith, I will live so long as I may, that's the certain of it; and when I cannot live any longer, I will do as I may: that is my rest,[2] that is the rendezvous of it.[3]

BARDOLPH.

It is certain, corporal, that he is married to Nell Quickly: and, certainly, she did you wrong; for you were troth-plight[4] to her.

NYM.

I cannot tell:—things must be as they may: men may sleep, and they may have their throats about them at that time; and, some say, knives have edges. It must be as it may: though patience be a tired mare,[5] yet she will plod. There must be conclusions. Well, I cannot tell.

BARDOLPH.

Here comes Ancient Pistol and his wife:—good corporal, be patient here.

Enter PISTOL *and* HOSTESS.

How now, mine host Pistol!

PISTOL.

Base tike,[6] call'st thou me host?[7]
Now, by this hand, I swear, I scorn the term;
Nor shall my Nell keep lodgers.

HOSTESS.

No, by my troth, not long; for we cannot lodge and board a dozen or fourteen gentlewomen that live honestly by the prick of their needles, but it will be thought we keep a bawdy-house straight.[8] [NYM *and* PISTOL *draw.*] O well-a-day, Lady,[9] if

---

[1] sworn brothers: knights who have taken a blood oath to stand together in their adventures. [2] my rest: my resolve; my last throw. [3] that is the rendezvous of it: that is my last resort. [4] troth-plight: betrothed. [5] patience be a tired mare: patience is wearing out. [6] tike: mongrel; cur. [7] host: owner of the tavern through his marriage to Mistress Quickly. [8] straight: immediately. [9] Lady: by Our Lady (a mild oath).

he be not drawn now! We shall see wilful adultery and murder committed.

BARDOLPH.

Good lieutenant,—good corporal,—offer nothing here.

NYM.

Pish!

PISTOL.

Pish for thee, Iceland dog![1] thou prick-ear'd[2] cur of Iceland!

HOSTESS.

Good Corporal Nym, show thy valour, and put up your sword.

NYM.

Will you shog off? [3] I would have you *solus*.[4]

PISTOL.

Solus, egregious dog? O viper vile!
The *solus* in thy most mervailous[5] face;
The *solus* in thy teeth, and in thy throat,
And in thy hateful lungs, yea, in thy maw,[6] perdy,[7]
And, which is worse, within thy nasty mouth!
I do retort the *solus* in thy bowels;
For I can take,[8] and Pistol's cock is up,[9]
And flashing fire will follow.

NYM.

I am not Barbason;[10] you cannot conjure me. I have an humour to knock you indifferently well. If you grow fowl with me, Pistol, I will scour you with my rapier, as I may, in fair terms: if you would walk off, I would prick your guts a little, in good terms, as I may: and that's the humour of it.

---

[1] Iceland dog: curly-haired lapdog.   [2] prick-ear'd: with pricked-up ears.   [3] shog off: jog off.   [4] *solus*: alone (not understanding the French word, Pistol takes it as an insult).   [5] mervailous: marvelous.   [6] maw: stomach.   [7] perdy: *per Dieu;* by God (a mild oath).   [8] I can take: I can take umbrage.   [9] cock is up: i.e., his lever is ready for firing.   [10] Barbason: the name of a demon.

PISTOL.

O braggart vile, and damned furious wight! [1]
The grave doth gape, and doting death is near;
Therefore exhale.[2]

BARDOLPH.

Hear me, hear me what I say:—he that strikes the first stroke,
I'll run him up to the hilts, as I am a soldier.   [Draws.

PISTOL.

An oath of mickle[3] might; and fury shall abate.—
Give me thy fist, thy fore-foot to me give:
Thy spirits are most tall.[4]   [They sheathe their swords.

NYM.

I will cut thy throat, one time or other, in fair terms: that is
the humour of it.

PISTOL.

Couple a gorge! [5]
That is the word. I thee defy again.
O hound of Crete,[6] think'st thou my spouse to get?
No; to the spital[7] go,
And from the powdering-tub[8] of infamy
Fetch forth the lazar kite of Cressid's kind,[9]
Doll Tearsheet[10] she by name, and her espouse:
I have, and I will hold, the *quondam*[11] Quickly
For the only she; and—*pauca*,[12] there's enough.
Go to.

Enter BOY.

BOY.

Mine host Pistol, you must come to my master,—and you,
hostess:—he is very sick, and would to bed.—Good Bardolph,
put thy face between his sheets, and do the office of a warm-
ing-pan.—Faith, he's very ill.

---

[1] wight: fellow.   [2] exhale: die; draw your last breath.   [3] mickle:
a great amount.   [4] tall: valiant.   [5] *Couple a gorge:* Pistol's gar-
bled French for *couper la gorge*—"slit a throat."   [6] hound of
Crete: bloodhound.   [7] spital: hospital.   [8] powdering-tub: a
treatment for venereal disease.   [9] lazar . . . kind: an allusion to
Cressida; lazar: leper; kite: bird of the crow family.   [10] Doll
Tearsheet: see II *Henry IV.*   [11] *quondam:* former.   [12] *pauca:*
in a few words.

BARDOLPH.

Away, you rogue!

HOSTESS.

By my troth, he'll yield the crow a pudding[1] one of these days:
the king has kill'd his heart.[2]—Good husband, come home
presently.   [*Exeunt* HOSTESS *and* BOY.

BARDOLPH.

Come, shall I make you two friends? We must to France together: why the devil should we keep knives to cut one another's throats?

PISTOL.

Let floods o'erswell, and fiends for food howl on!

NYM.

You'll pay me the eight shillings I won of you at betting?

PISTOL.

Base is the slave that pays.

NYM.

That now I will have: that's the humour of it.

PISTOL.

As manhood shall compound:[3] push home.   [*They draw.*

BARDOLPH.

By this sword, he that makes the first thrust, I'll kill him; by
this sword, I will.   [*Draws.*

PISTOL.

Sword is an oath, and oaths must have their course.

BARDOLPH.

Corporal Nym, an[4] thou wilt be friends, be friends: an thou

---

[1] yield the crow a pudding: become carrion flesh on the gallows;
i.e., die.   [2] his heart: Falstaff's heart.   [3] As manhood shall compound: the way men must settle their debts.   [4] an: if.

wilt not, why, then be enemies with me too. Prithee, put up.[1]

NYM.

I shall have my eight shillings I won of you at betting?

PISTOL.

A noble[2] shalt thou have, and present pay;[3]
And liquor likewise will I give to thee,
And friendship shall combine and brotherhood;
I'll live by Nym, and Nym shall live by me;—
Is not this just?—for I shall sutler[4] be
Unto the camp, and profits will accrue.
Give me thy hand.   [*They sheathe their swords.*

NYM.

I shall have my noble?

PISTOL.

In cash most justly paid.

NYM.

Well, then, that's the humour of it.

Enter HOSTESS.

HOSTESS.

As ever you came of women, come in quickly to Sir John. Ah,
poor heart! he is so shaked of a burning quotidian tertian,[5]
that it is most lamentable to behold. Sweet men, come to him.

NYM.

The king hath run bad humours on the knight, that's the
even[6] of it.

PISTOL.

Nym, thou hast spoke the right;
His heart is fracted and corroborate.[7]

NYM.

The king is a good king: but it must be as it may; he passes
some humours and careers.[8]

---

[1] put up: sheathe your sword.   [2] noble: 6s 8d.   [3] present pay:
immediate payment.   [4] sutler: provisioner to the army.   [5] quotidian tertian: she is mixed up on her medical terms; quotidian is
a fever recurring every day, a tertian every three days.   [6] even:
plain truth.   [7] fracted and corroborate: Pistol's term for *broken*.
[8] careers: a term in horsemanship for short gallops to and fro;
therefore, the king is impulsive, or capricious.

PISTOL.

Let us condole the knight; for, lambkins,[1] we will live.

[*Exeunt.*

SCENE II.

Southampton. A council-chamber.

Enter EXETER, BEDFORD, *and* WESTMORELAND.

DUKE OF BEDFORD.

'Fore God, his Grace is bold, to trust these traitors.

DUKE OF EXETER.

They shall be apprehended by and by.[2]

EARL OF WESTMORELAND.

How smooth and even[3] they do bear themselves!
As if allegiance in their bosoms sat,
Crowned with faith and constant loyalty.

DUKE OF BEDFORD.

The king hath note of all that they intend,
By interception which they dream not of.

DUKE OF EXETER.

Nay, but the man that was his bedfellow,[4]
Whom he hath dull'd[5] and cloy'd with gracious favours,
That he should, for a foreign purse, so sell
His sovereign's life to death and treachery!

Trumpets sound. Enter KING HENRY, CAMBRIDGE, SCROOP,
GREY, LORDS, *and* ATTENDANTS.

KING HENRY.

Now sits the wind fair, and we will aboard.
My Lord of Cambridge,—and my kind Lord of Masham,—

---

[1] lambkins: little lambs (a term of endearment).
[2] by and by: soon.
[3] even: calmly.
[4] bedfellow: Scroop.
[5] dull'd: bored; tired.

And you, my gentle knight,—give me your thoughts:
Think you not that the powers[1] we bear with us
Will cut their passage through the force of France,
Doing the execution and the act
For which we have in head[2] assembled them?

    LORD SCROOP.

No doubt, my liege, if each man do his best.

    KING HENRY.

I doubt not that; since we are well persuaded
We carry not a heart with us from hence
That grows not in a fair consent[3] with ours,
Nor leave not one behind that doth not wish
Success and conquest to attend on us.

    EARL OF CAMBRIDGE.

Never was monarch better fear'd and loved
Than is your majesty: there's not, I think, a subject
That sits in heart-grief[4] and uneasiness
Under the sweet shade of your government.

    SIR THOMAS GREY.

True: those that were your father's enemies
Have steept their galls[5] in honey, and do serve you
With hearts create[6] of duty and of zeal.

    KING HENRY.

We therefore have great cause of thankfulness;
And shall forget the office of our hand,[7]
Sooner than quittance[8] of desert and merit
According to the weight and worthiness.

    LORD SCROOP.

So service shall with steeled sinews[9] toil,
And labour shall refresh itself with hope,
To do your Grace incessant services.

---

[1] powers: armies.   [2] in head: in full force.   [3] a fair consent:
complete agreement.   [4] heart-grief: sorrow.   [5] galls: bitterness.
[6] create: made only.   [7] office of our hand: use of our hands.
[8] quittance: payment.   [9] steeled sinews: renewed vigor.

KING HENRY.

We judge no less.—Uncle of Exeter,
Enlarge[1] the man committed yesterday,
That rail'd against[2] our person: we consider
It was excess of wine that set him on;
And, on his more advice,[3] we pardon him.

LORD SCROOP.

That's mercy, but too much security:[4]
Let him be punisht, sovereign; lest example
Breed, by his sufferance,[5] more of such a kind.

KING HENRY.

O, let us yet be merciful.

EARL OF CAMBRIDGE.

So may your highness, and yet punish too.

SIR THOMAS GREY.

Sir, you show great mercy, if you give him life,
After the taste of much correction.

KING HENRY.

Alas, your too much love and care of me
Are heavy orisons[6] 'gainst this poor wretch!
If little faults, proceeding on distemper,[7]
Shall not be winkt at, how shall we stretch our eye[8]
When capital crimes, chew'd, swallow'd, and digested,
Appear before us?—We'll yet enlarge that man,
Though Cambridge, Scroop, and Grey, in their dear care
And tender preservation of our person,
Would have him punisht. And now to our French causes:
Who are the late[9] commissioners?

---

[1] Enlarge: free; set at liberty.   [2] rail'd against: spoke out against.
[3] on his more advice: on his thinking better of it.   [4] security:
overconfidence.   [5] by his sufferance: by your failure to punish
him; by your toleration of him.   [6] heavy orisons: weighty
prayers.   [7] proceeding on distemper: arising from drunkenness.
[8] stretch our eye: stare in horror.   [9] late: lately appointed.

EARL OF CAMBRIDGE.

I one, my lord:
Your highness bade me ask for it to-day.

LORD SCROOP.

So did you me, my liege.

SIR THOMAS GREY.

And me, my royal sovereign.

KING HENRY.

Then Richard earl of Cambridge, there is yours;—
There yours, Lord Scroop of Masham;—and, sir knight,
Grey of Northumberland, this same is yours:—
Read them; and know, I know your worthiness.—
My Lord of Westmoreland, and uncle Exeter,
We will aboard to-night.—Why, how now, gentlemen!
What see you in those papers, that you lose
So much complexion? [1]—Look ye, how they change!
Their cheeks are paper. [2]—Why, what read you there,
That hath so cowarded [3] and chased your blood
Out of appearance?

EARL OF CAMBRIDGE.

             I do confess my fault;
And do submit me to your highness' mercy.

SIR THOMAS GREY *and* LORD SCROOP.

To which we all appeal.

KING HENRY.

The mercy that was quick [4] in us but late,
By your own counsel is supprest and kill'd:
You must not dare, for shame, to talk of mercy;
For your own reasons [5] turn into your bosoms,

---

[1] lose/So much complexion: turn so pale.
[2] paper: as white as paper.
[3] so cowarded: made such a coward of you.
[4] quick: alive.
[5] reasons: arguments.

As dogs upon their masters, worrying you.—
See you, my princes and my noble peers,
These English monsters! My Lord of Cambridge here,—
You know how apt our love was to accord[1]
To furnish him with all appertinents[2]
Belonging to his honour; and this man
Hath, for a few light crowns, lightly conspired,
And sworn unto the practices[3] of France,
To kill us here in Hampton:[4] to the which
This knight, no less for bounty bound to us
Than Cambridge is, hath likewise sworn.—But, O,
What shall I say to thee, Lord Scroop? thou cruel,
Ingrateful,[5] savage, and inhuman creature!
Thou that didst bear the key of all my counsels,
That knew'st the very bottom of my soul,[6]
That almost mightst have coin'd me into gold,
Wouldst thou have practised on me for thy use,—
May it be possible, that foreign hire
Could out of thee extract one spark of evil
That might annoy[7] my finger? 'tis so strange,
That, though the truth of it stands off as gross[8]
As black from white, my eye will scarcely see it.
Treason and murder ever[9] kept together,
As two yoke-devils sworn to either's purpose,
Working so grossly in a natural cause,
That admiration[10] did not whoop[11] at them:
But thou, 'gainst all proportion,[12] didst bring in
Wonder to wait on treason and on murder:
And whatsoever cunning fiend it was
That wrought upon thee so preposterously,[13]
Hath got the voice[14] in hell for excellence:
And other devils, that suggest by treasons,
Do botch and bungle up damnation

---

[1] accord: agree. [2] appertinents: appurtenances. [3] practices:
plots. [4] Hampton: Southampton. [5] Ingrateful: ungrateful.
[6] the very bottom of my soul: my most intimate secrets. [7] annoy:
harm. [8] gross: obvious. [9] ever: always. [10] admiration: wonder. [11] whoop: cry out. [12] 'gainst all proportion: against every
natural instinct. [13] preposterously: unnaturally. [14] voice: vote.

With patches, colours, and with forms being fetcht
From glistering semblances of piety;[1]
But he that temper'd thee[2] bade thee stand up,[3]
Gave thee no instance[4] why thou shouldst do treason,
Unless to dub thee with[5] the name of traitor.
If that same demon that hath gull'd[6] thee thus
Should with his lion-gait[7] walk the whole world,
He might return to vasty Tartar[8] back,
And tell the legions, 'I can never win
A soul so easy as that Englishman's.'
O, how hast thou with jealousy[9] infected
The sweetness of affiance! [10] Show men dutiful?
Why, so didst thou: seem they grave and learned?
Why, so didst thou: come they of noble family?
Why, so didst thou: seem they religious?
Why, so didst thou: or are they spare in diet;
Free from gross passion, or of mirth or anger;
Constant in spirit, not swerving with the blood;[11]
Garnisht and deckt in modest complement;[12]
Not working with the eye without the ear,
And but in purged judgement[13] trusting neither?
Such and so finely bolted[14] didst thou seem:
And thus thy fall hath left a kind of blot,
To mark the full-fraught[15] man and best indued[16]
With some suspicion. I will weep for thee;
For this revolt of thine, methinks, is like
Another fall of man.—Their faults are open:
Arrest them to the answer of the law;—
And God acquit them of their practices!

DUKE OF EXETER.

I arrest thee of high treason, by the name of
Richard earl of Cambridge.

---

[1] botch . . . piety: attempt to patch up every monstrous deed by
a pious appearance. [2] temper'd thee: molded you. [3] stand up:
i.e., as a complete man. [4] instance: reason. [5] dub thee with:
bestow on you. [6] gull'd: deceived. [7] lion-gait: see Peter 5:8.
[8] vasty Tartar: the vast wastes of hell (Tartarus). [9] jealousy: suspicion. [10] affiance: confidence. [11] the blood: passion. [12] complement: that is, the appearance of a nobleman. [13] purged judgement: after careful consideration. [14] bolted: sifted; free of blem-
ishes. [15] full-fraught: gifted. [16] indued: endowed.

I arrest thee of high treason, by the name of
Henry Lord Scroop of Masham.
I arrest thee of high treason, by the name of
Thomas Grey, knight, of Northumberland.

LORD SCROOP.

Our purposes God justly hath discover'd;[1]
And I repent my fault more than my death;
Which I beseech your highness to forgive,
Although my body pay the price of it.

EARL OF CAMBRIDGE.

For me,—the gold of France did not seduce;
Although I did admit it as a motive
The sooner to effect what I intended:[2]
But God be thanked for prevention;
Which I in sufferance[3] heartily will rejoice,
Beseeching God and you to pardon me.

SIR THOMAS GREY.

Never did faithful subject more rejoice
At the discovery of most dangerous treason
Than I do at this hour joy o'er myself,
Prevented from a damned enterprise:
My fault, but not my body, pardon, sovereign.

KING HENRY.

God quit you in his mercy! Hear your sentence.
You have conspired against our royal person,
Join'd with an enemy proclaim'd, and from his coffers
Received the golden earnest[4] of our death;
Wherein you would have sold your king to slaughter,
His princes and his peers to servitude,
His subjects to oppression and contempt,
And his whole kingdom into desolation.
Touching our person,[5] seek we no revenge;

---

[1] discover'd: revealed; uncovered.
[2] what I intended: his purpose was to secure the throne for the Earl of March.
[3] sufferance: suffering; atonement.
[4] golden earnest: payment of gold as a pledge of the bargain.
[5] Touching our person: as for myself personally.

But we our kingdom's safety must so tender,[1]
Whose ruin you have sought, that to her laws
We do deliver you. Get you, therefore, hence,
Poor miserable wretches,[2] to your death:
The taste whereof, God of his mercy give
You patience to endure, and true repentance
Of all your dear[3] offences!—Bear them hence.

    [*Exeunt* CAMBRIDGE, SCROOP, *and* GREY, *guarded.*

Now, lords, for France; the enterprise whereof
Shall be to you as us like[4] glorious.
We doubt not of a fair and lucky war,
Since God so graciously hath brought to light
This dangerous treason, lurking in our way
To hinder our beginnings; we doubt not now
But every rub[5] is smoothed on our way.
Then, forth, dear countrymen: let us deliver
Our puissance into the hand of God,
Putting it straight[6] in expedition.[7]
Cheerly[8] to sea; the signs of war[9] advance:
No king of England, if not king of France.   [*Exeunt.*

SCENE III.

London. Before the Boar's-Head Tavern, Eastcheap.

Enter PISTOL, HOSTESS, NYM, BARDOLPH, *and* BOY.

HOSTESS.
Prithee, honey-sweet husband, let me bring[10] thee to Staines.[11]
    PISTOL.
No; for my manly heart doth yearn.—[12]

---

[1] tender: cherish; preserve.   [2] wretches: condemned criminals.
[3] dear: grievous.   [4] like: alike.   [5] rub: hindrance; obstacle.
[6] straight: immediately.   [7] in expedition: on the march.
[8] Cheerly: cheerfully.   [9] signs of war: banners; standards.
[10] bring: escort.   [11] Staines: Staines Bridge over the Thames, the
first stage stop on the road to Southampton.   [12] yearn: grieve.

Bardolph, be blithe;—Nym, rouse thy vaunting veins;—[1]
Boy, bristle thy courage up;—for Falstaff he is dead,
And we must yearn therefore.

BARDOLPH.

Would I were with him, wheresome'er he is, either in heaven
or in hell!

HOSTESS.

Nay, sure, he's not in hell: he's in Arthur's bosom,[2] if ever man
went to Arthur's bosom. A'[3] made a finer end, and went away,
an it[4] had been any christom child;[5] a' parted[6] ev'n just between twelve and one, ev'n at the turning o' th' tide: for after
I saw him fumble with the sheets, and play with flowers, and
smile upon his fingers' ends, I knew there was but one way;[7]
for his nose was as sharp as a pen,[8] and a' babbled of green
fields. 'How now, Sir John!' quoth I: 'what, man! be o' good
cheer.' So a' cried out 'God, God, God!' three or four times.
Now I, to comfort him, bid him a' should not think of God; I
hoped there was no need to trouble himself with any such
thoughts yet. So a' bade me lay more clothes on his feet: I
put my hand into the bed and felt them, and they were as cold
as any stone; then I felt to his knees, and they were as cold as
any stone; and so upward and upward, and all was as cold
as any stone.

NYM.

They say he cried out of sack.[9]

HOSTESS.

Ay, that a' did.

---

[1] rouse thy vaunting veins: call forth your usual boastful spirits.
[2] Arthur's bosom: Mistress Quickly (now Mrs. Pistol) means "Abra-
ham's bosom." 　[3] A': he. 　[4] an it: as if he. 　[5] christom child: a
newly baptized child and therefore, innocent. 　[6] parted: departed;
it was an old superstition that many died just as the tide started to
ebb. 　[7] but one way: i.e., only death. 　[8] as sharp as a pen: as
white as a goose quill. 　[9] cried out of sack: cried out against the
evils of wine (drinking).

BARDOLPH.

And of women.

HOSTESS.

Nay, that a' did not.

BOY.

Yes, that a' did; and said they were devils incarnate.

HOSTESS.

A' could never abide carnation;[1] 'twas a colour he never liked.

BOY.

A' said once, the devil would have him about women.[2]

HOSTESS.

A' did in some sort, indeed, handle women; but then he was rheumatic,[3] and talkt of the whore of Babylon.

BOY.

Do you not remember, a' saw a flea stick upon Bardolph's nose, and a' said it was a black soul[4] burning in hell-fire?

BARDOLPH.

Well, the fuel[5] is gone that maintain'd that fire: that's all the riches I got in his service.

NYM.

Shall we shog?[6] the king will be gone from Southampton.

PISTOL.

Come, let's away.— My love, give me thy lips.
Look to my chattels and my movables:
Let senses rule;[7] the word is 'Pitch and pay;'[8]
Trust none;
For oaths are straws, men's faiths are wafer-cakes,[9]

---

[1] carnation: Mrs. Quickly confuses *incarnate* with *carnation*, a flesh color. [2] about women: because of his weakness for women. [3] rheumatic: delirious. [4] black soul: lost soul. [5] fuel: whisky. [6] shog: be off. [7] Let senses rule: keep your wits about you. [8] 'Pitch and pay': pay on the spot; no credit. [9] wafer-cakes: brittle and easily broken.

And hold-fast is the only dog,[1] my duck:
Therefore, *caveto*[2] be thy counsellor.
Go, clear thy crystals.[3]—Yoke-fellows in arms,
Let us to France; like horse-leeches, my boys,
To suck, to suck, the very blood to suckl

BOY.

And that's but unwholesome food, they say.

PISTOL.

Touch her soft mouth, and march.

BARDOLPH.

Farewell, hostess.   [*Kissing her.*

NYM.

I cannot kiss, that is the humour of it; but, adieu.

PISTOL.

Let housewifery appear:[4] keep close,[5] I thee command.

HOSTESS.

Farewell; adieu.   [*Exeunt.*

SCENE IV.

France. A room in the French KING's palace.

Flourish.[6] *Enter the French* KING, *the* DAUPHIN, *the* DUKE OF
BURGUNDY, *the* CONSTABLE,[7] *and others.*

FRENCH KING.

Thus comes the English with full power upon us;
And more than carefully it us concerns
To answer royally in our defences.
Therefore the Dukes of Berri and of Bretagne,
Of Brabant and of Orleans, shall make forth,—
And you, Prince Dauphin,—with all swift dispatch,

---

[1] hold-fast is the only dog: from the proverbial saying, "Brag is a good dog, but Hold-fast is better."   [2] *caveto*: from the Latin *caveo*; caution; take care.   [3] clear thy crystals: wipe your eyes.   [4] Let housewifery appear: let good management (thrift) take over.   [5] keep close: keep the doors locked, or guard your tongue.   [6] *Flourish*: fanfare.   [7] Constable: one of the principal officers in the royal household.

To line and new repair[1] our towns of war
With men of courage and with means defendant;[2]
For England[3] his approaches makes as fierce
As waters to the sucking of a gulf.[4]
It fits[5] us, then, to be as provident
As fear may teach us, out of late examples[6]
Left by the fatal and neglected[7] English
Upon our fields.

    DAUPHIN.

              My most redoubted father,
It is most meet[8] we arm us 'gainst the foe;
For peace itself should not so dull a kingdom,
Though war nor no known quarrel were in question,
But that defences, musters, preparations,
Should be maintain'd, assembled, and collected,
As were a war[9] in expectation.
Therefore, I say 'tis meet we all go forth
To view the sick and feeble parts of France:
And let us do it with no show of fear;
No, with no more than if we heard that England
Were busied with a Whitsun morris-dance:[10]
For, my good liege, she is so idly king'd,[11]
Her sceptre so fantastically borne
By a vain, giddy, shallow, humorous[12] youth,
That fear attends her not.

    CONSTABLE OF FRANCE.

              O peace, Prince Dauphin!
You are too much mistaken in this king:
Question your Grace the late ambassadors,—
With what great state he heard their embassy,
How well supplied with noble counsellors,

---

[1] line and new repair: reinforce.   [2] means defendant: all the means of defense.   [3] England: the King of England.   [4] gulf: whirlpool.   [5] fits: befits.   [6] late examples: the English victories at Crécy and Poitiers.   [7] fatal and neglected: deadly and underestimated.   [8] meet: fitting.   [9] As were a war: as if a war were.   [10] Whitsun morris-dance: folk dancing in the open, usually in early summer (Whitsuntide) and on May Day.   [11] so idly king'd: ruled by such an empty-headed king.   [12] humorous: capricious.

How modest in exception,[1] and withal
How terrible in constant[2] resolution,—
And you shall find his vanities forespent[3]
Were but the outside of the Roman Brutus,[4]
Covering discretion with a coat of folly;
As gardeners do with ordure[5] hide those roots
That shall first spring and be most delicate.

DAUPHIN.

Well, 'tis not so, my lord high-constable;
But though we think it so, it is no matter:
In cases of defence 'tis best to weigh
The enemy more mighty than he seems:
So the proportions of defence are fill'd;
Which, of a weak and niggardly projection,
Doth, like a miser, spoil his coat with scanting[6]
A little cloth.

FRENCH KING.

Think we King Harry strong;
And princes, look you strongly arm to meet him.
The kindred of him hath been flesht[7] upon us;
And he is bred out of that bloody strain[8]
That haunted[9] us in our familiar paths:
Witness our too-much memorable shame
When Cressy[10] battle fatally was struck,
And all our princes captived by the hand
Of that black name, Edward, Black Prince of Wales;
Whiles that his mountain sire,[11]—on mountain standing,
Up in the air, crown'd with the golden sun,—
Saw his heroical seed, and smiled to see him,
Mangle the work of nature, and deface
The patterns that by God and by French fathers

---

[1] in exception: when he took exception; in disagreement. [2] constant: unshaken. [3] vanities forespent: former frivolous behavior.
[4] the Roman Brutus: Lucius Junius Brutus, who feigned madness in order to free Rome from the Tarquins. [5] ordure: manure; fertilizer. [6] scanting: saving. [7] hath been flesht: has already tasted first blood. [8] strain: race. [9] haunted: pursued. [10] Cressy: Crécy. [11] his mountain sire: Edward III, who was born in the mountains of Wales.

Had twenty years been made. This is a stem
Of that victorious stock; and let us fear
The native mightiness and fate of him.[1]

Enter a MESSENGER.

MESSENGER.
Ambassadors from Harry king of England
Do crave admittance to your majesty.
    FRENCH KING.
We'll give them present[2] audience. Go, and bring them.
                   [*Exeunt* MESSENGER *and certain* LORDS.
You see this chase is hotly follow'd, friends.
    DAUPHIN.
Turn head, and stop pursuit; for coward dogs
Most spend their mouths,[3] when what they seem to threaten
Runs far before them. Good my sovereign,[4]
Take up the English short;[5] and let them know
Of what a monarchy you are the head:
Self-love, my liege, is not so vile a sin
As self-neglecting.

Enter LORDS, *with* EXETER *and* TRAIN.

    FRENCH KING.
              From our brother England?
    DUKE OF EXETER.
From him; and thus he greets your majesty.
He wills you, in the name of God Almighty,
That you divest yourself, and lay apart
The borrow'd glories, that, by gift of heaven,
By law of nature and of nations, 'longs[6]
To him and to his heirs; namely, the crown,
And all wide-stretched honours that pertain,
By custom and the ordinance of times,[7]

---

[1] native mightiness and fate of him: "great good fortune ordained by destiny"—Schmidt.   [2] present: immediate.   [3] Most spend their mouths: bark the most (in hunting).   [4] Good my sovereign: my good sovereign.   [5] Take up the English short: i.e., make short shrift of them.   [6] 'longs: belongs.   [7] the ordinance of times: the laws and customs of past ages.

Unto the crown of France. That you may know
'Tis no sinister[1] nor no awkward[2] claim,
Pickt from the worm-holes of long-vanisht days,
Nor from the dust of old oblivion raked,
He sends you this most memorable line,[3]

[Gives a paper.

In every branch truly demonstrative;
Willing you overlook[4] this pedigree:
And when you find him evenly[5] derived
From his most famed of famous ancestors,
Edward the Third, he bids you then resign
Your crown and kingdom, indirectly[6] held
From him the native and true challenger.[7]

FRENCH KING.

Or else what follows?

DUKE OF EXETER.

Bloody constraint; for if you hide the crown
Even in your hearts, there will he rake for it:
Therefore in fierce tempest is he coming,
In thunder and in earthquake, like a Jove,
That, if requiring[8] fail, he will compel;
And bids you, in the bowels of the Lord,[9]
Deliver up the crown; and to take mercy
On the poor souls for whom this hungry war
Opens his vasty[10] jaws: and on your head
Turns he the widows' tears, the orphans' cries,
The dead men's blood, the pining maidens' groans,
For husbands, fathers, and betrothed lovers,
That shall be swallow'd in this controversy.
This is his claim, his threatening, and my message;
Unless the Dauphin be in presence here,
To whom expressly I bring greeting too.

---

[1] sinister: illegitimate.   [2] awkward: perverse.   [3] line: pedigree;
family chart.   [4] overlook: peruse; read.   [5] evenly: directly.
[6] indirectly: not by direct line of descent.   [7] the native and true
challenger: the true claimant to the throne of France by right of
birth.   [8] requiring: demanding; asking.   [9] in the bowels of the
Lord: by Divine mercy.   [10] vasty: vast; immense.

FRENCH KING.

For us, we will consider of this further:
To-morrow shall you bear our full intent
Back to our brother England.

DAUPHIN.

For the Dauphin,
I stand here for him: what to him from England?

DUKE OF EXETER.

Scorn and defiance; slight regard, contempt,
And any thing that may not misbecome
The mighty sender, doth he prize you at.
Thus says my king: an if[1] your father's highness
Do not, in grant of all demands at large,[2]
Sweeten the bitter mock you sent his majesty,
He'll call you to so hot an answer of it,
That caves and womby[3] vaultages of France
Shall chide your trespass, and return your mock
In second accent[4] of his ordnance.[5]

DAUPHIN.

Say, if my father render fair return,
It is against my will; for I desire
Nothing but odds[6] with England: to that end,
As matching to his youth and vanity,
I did present him with the Paris balls.[7]

DUKE OF EXETER.

He'll make your Paris Louvre[8] shake for it,
Were it the mistress-court of mighty Europe:
And, be assured, you'll find a difference,
As we, his subjects, have in wonder found,
Between the promise of his greener[9] days
And these he masters[10] now: now he weighs time,
Even to the utmost grain:—that you shall read
In your own losses, if he stay in France.

---

[1] an if: if.   [2] at large: in full.   [3] womby: hollow.   [4] second accent: echo.   [5] ordnance: cannon.   [6] odds: disagreement.   [7] Paris balls: tennis balls.   [8] Louvre: with a play on the word "lover."   [9] greener: younger.   [10] masters: possesses.

FRENCH KING.

To-morrow shall you know our mind at full.[1]

DUKE OF EXETER.

Dispatch us with all speed, lest that our king
Come here himself to question our delay;
For he is footed[2] in this land already.

FRENCH KING.

You shall be soon dispatcht with fair conditions
A night is but small breath and little pause
To answer matters of this consequence.

[Flourish. Exeunt.

---

[1] our mind in full: our full intentions.
[2] is footed: has landed.

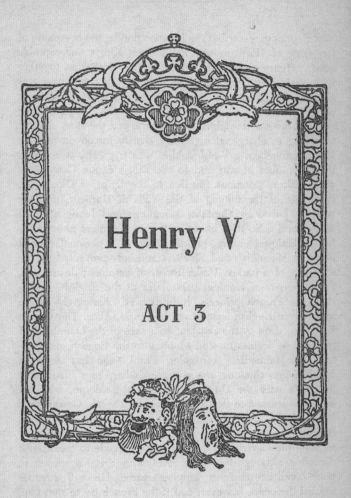

Henry V

ACT 3

THE PROLOGUE describes the invasion flotilla, the beginning of the siege of Harfleur, and the French King's unacceptable offer to Henry of the hand of his daughter Katharine, together with some petty dukedoms as a dowry. Scene i opens as Henry exhorts his soldiers to charge the walls of Halfleur once more; with a sudden drop from the King's stirring rhetoric, we see Bardolph, Nym, Pistol, and the Boy, all most unwilling to charge, though very shortly forced onward by Captain Fluellen, a Welsh soldier who is greatly devoted to the techniques of war and to the King's cause. Gower, another officer, summons Fluellen to the Duke of Gloucester, in charge of the mining of the walls of Harfleur, and the two are joined by Captains Macmorris and Jamy, an Irish soldier and a Scottish one. Shortly, an argument about military techniques ensues, rapidly rising to a personal quarrel between Macmorris and Fluellen, and only prevented by the sounding of a parley. Under threat of imminent destruction, the Governor of Harfleur capitulates to the English. Katharine, the French princess, is introduced charmingly in the midst of an English lesson from her nurse, Alice. The French King, urged on by the arrogant assurance of the Dauphin and the nobles, decides to send Montjoy to the English, demanding their immediate surrender. Pistol, who has deceived Fluellen into thinking him a brave soldier, begs Fluellen to intercede with the Duke of Exeter for Bardolph, who has been condemned to death for robbing a church. Gower gives Fluellen the true picture of such soldiers as Pistol and Bardolph, and the King sternly approves the execution of all such plunderers. He then refuses to accede to the French demands, although he admits to Montjoy that his army is in poor condition and his supplies scarce. He will advance toward the coast, however, and if the French try to stop him, he will fight. In contrast, the assured French are spoiling for a fight; the final scene shows them exchanging boasts about their prowess and their coming victory, and longing for dawn when they will attack the English forces.

ACT III. PROLOGUE.

Enter CHORUS.

CHORUS.

Thus with imagined wing[1] our swift scene flies,
In motion of no less celerity
Than that of thought. Suppose that you have seen
The well-appointed[2] king at Hampton[3] pier
Embark his royalty; and his brave[4] fleet
With silken streamers the young Phœbus[5] fanning:
Play with your fancies; and in them behold
Upon the hempen tackle ship-boys climbing;
Hear the shrill whistle which doth order give
To sounds confused; behold the threaden[6] sails,
Borne with th'invisible and creeping wind,
Draw the huge bottoms[7] through the furrow'd sea,
Breasting the lofty surge: O, do but think
You stand upon the rivage[8] and behold
A city on th'inconstant billows dancing;
For so appears this fleet majestical,
Holding due course to Harfleur. Follow, follow!
Grapple your minds to sternage[9] of this navy;

---

[1] with imagined wing: on the wings of imagination. [2] well-appointed: well-equipped. [3] Hampton: Southampton. [4] brave: splendid. [5] young Phœbus: the morning sun; Phœbus—the sun god. [6] threaden: i.e., woven of thread. [7] bottoms: ships. [8] rivage: shore. [9] Grapple your minds to sternage: fix your minds on the stern; that is, follow the story.

And leave your England, as dead midnight still,
Guarded with grandsires, babies, and old women,
Either past, or not arrived to, pith and puissance;[1]
For who is he, whose chin is but enricht
With one appearing hair, that will not follow
These cull'd[2] and choice-drawn[3] cavaliers to France?
Work, work your thoughts, and therein see a siege;
Behold the ordnance on their carriages,
With fatal mouths gaping on girded[4] Harfleur.
Suppose th'ambassador from the French comes back;
Tells Harry that the king doth offer him
Katharine his daughter; and with her, to dowry,[5]
Some petty and unprofitable dukedoms.
The offer likes not: and the nimble gunner
With linstock[6] now the devilish cannon touches,
                    [*Alarum, and chambers go off, within.*
And down goes all before them. Still be kind,
And eke out our performance with your mind.   [*Exit.*

SCENE I.

France. Before Harfleur.

Alarums.[7] *Enter* KING HENRY, EXETER, BEDFORD, GLOSTER, *and*
SOLDIERS, *with scaling-ladders.*

KING HENRY.
Once more unto the breach, dear friends, once more;
Or close the wall up with our English dead!

---

[1] pith and puissance: full strength.   [2] cull'd: hand-picked.
[3] choice-drawn: carefully chosen from the best.   [4] girded: surrounded.   [5] to dowry: as her dowry.   [6] linstock: a long staff for
lighting the cannon.   [7] *Alarums:* noise of battle.

In peace there's nothing so becomes a man
As modest stillness and humility:
But when the blast of war blows in our ears,
Then imitate the action of the tiger;
Stiffen the sinews, summon up the blood,
Disguise fair nature[1] with hard-favour'd[2] rage:
Then lend the eye a terrible aspect;
Let it pry through the portage[3] of the head
Like the brass cannon; let the brow o'erwhelm it
As fearfully as doth a galled[4] rock
O'erhang and jutty[5] his confounded base,[6]
Swill'd with[7] the wild and wasteful ocean.
Now set the teeth, and stretch the nostril wide;
Hold hard the breath, and bend up every spirit
To his full height!—On, on, you noble English,
Whose blood is fet[8] from fathers of war-proof!—[9]
Fathers that, like so many Alexanders,
Have in these parts from morn till even fought,
And sheathed their swords for lack of argument:—[10]
Dishonour not your mothers; now attest
That those whom you call'd fathers did beget you!
Be copy now to men of grosser blood,
And teach them how to war!—And you, good yeomen,[11]
Whose limbs were made in England, show us here
The mettle of your pasture;[12] let us swear
That you are worth your breeding: which I doubt not;
For there is none of you so mean and base,
That hath not noble lustre in your eyes.
I see you stand like greyhounds in the slips,[13]

---

[1] fair nature: your naturally good-natured appearance.   [2] hard-favour'd: stern-faced; hard-featured.   [3] portage: porthole; eye-sockets.   [4] galled: eroded by the waves.   [5] jutty: jutting over.   [6] his confounded base: its destroyed foundation.   [7] Swill'd with: swallowed by.   [8] fet: fetched.   [9] of war-proof: proved in battle.   [10] argument: opposition.   [11] yeomen: farmers.   [12] The mettle of your pasture: the quality of your background.   [13] in the slips: on their leashes.

Straining upon the start.[1] The game's afoot:
Follow your spirit; and, upon this charge,
Cry 'God for Harry, England, and Saint George!' [2]

       [Exeunt. Alarum, and chambers go off, within.

SCENE II.

The same.

Enter NYM, BARDOLPH, PISTOL, *and* BOY.

BARDOLPH.

On, on, on, on, on! to the breach, to the breach!

NYM.

Pray thee, corporal, stay: the knocks are too hot; and, for
mine own part, I have not a case[3] of lives: the humour of it is
too hot, that it is the very plain-song[4] of it.

PISTOL.

The plain-song is most just; for humours do abound;
Knocks go and come; God's vassals drop and die;
         And sword and shield,
           In bloody field,
       Doth win immortal fame.

BOY.

Would I were in an alehouse in London! I would give all my
fame for a pot of ale and safety.

PISTOL.

And I:
       If wishes would prevail with me,
       My purpose should not fail with me,
         But thither would I hie.[5]

---

[1] Straining upon the start: eager to begin the chase.
[2] Saint George: the patron saint of England.
[3] case: set; pair.
[4] plain-song: simple tune; therefore, simple truth.
[5] hie: hurry.

BOY.

> As duly, but not as truly,
>   As bird doth sing on bough.

Enter FLUELLEN.

FLUELLEN.

Got's plood!—[1] Up to the preaches,[2] you rascals! will you not
up to the preaches?   [*Driving them forward.*

PISTOL.

Be merciful, great duke, to men of mould![3]
Abate thy rage, abate thy manly rage!
Abate thy rage, great duke!
Good bawcock,[4] bate thy rage! use lenity, sweet chuck![5]

NYM.

These be good humours!—your honour runs bad humours.
[*Exeunt* NYM, BARDOLPH, *and* PISTOL *driven in by* FLUELLEN.

BOY.

As young as I am, I have observed these three swashers.[6] I
am boy[7] to them all three: but all they three, though they
would serve me, could not be man to me; for, indeed, three
such antics[8] do not amount to a man. For Bardolph,—he is
white-liver'd[9] and red-faced; by the means whereof a' faces
it out, but fights not. For Pistol,—he hath a killing tongue
and a quiet sword; by the means whereof a' breaks words,
and keeps whole weapons. For Nym,—he hath heard that
men of few words are the best men; and therefore he scorns
to say his prayers, lest a' should be thought a coward: but
his few bad words are matcht with as few good deeds; for a'
never broke any man's head but his own, and that was
against a post when he was drunk. They will steal any thing,

---

[1] plood: blood.   [2] preaches: breaches.   [3] men of mould: men of
common clay.   [4] bawcock: *beau coq;* a term of endearment (always masculine).   [5] chuck: chick (another term of endearment).
[6] swashers: swashbucklers; phonies.   [7] boy: servant.   [8] antics:
clowns.   [9] white-liver'd: cowardly.

and call it purchase.[1] Bardolph stole a lute-case, bore it
twelve leagues, and sold it for three-half-pence. Nym and
Bardolph are sworn brothers in filching; and in Calais they
stole a fire-shovel: I knew by that piece of service the men
would carry coals.[2] They would have me as familiar with
men's pockets as their gloves or their handkerchers: which
makes much against my manhood, if I should take from another's pocket to put into mine; for it is plain pocketing-up
of wrongs. I must leave them, and seek some better service:
their villainy goes against my weak stomach, and therefore I
must cast it up.   [*Exit.*

Enter FLUELLEN, GOWER *following.*

GOWER.

Captain Fluellen, you must come presently to the mines; the
Duke of Gloster would speak with you.

FLUELLEN.

To the mines! tell you the duke, it is not so goot to come
to the mines; for, look you, the mines is not according to
the disciplines of the war:[3] the concavities of it is not sufficient; for, look you, th'athversary—you may discuss unto the
duke, look you—is digt himself four yard under the counter-
mines:[4] by Cheshu,[5] I think a' will plow[6] up all, if there is
not petter[7] directions.

GOWER.

The Duke of Gloster, to whom the order of the siege is given,
is altogether directed by an Irishman,—a very valiant gentleman, i'faith.

---

[1] purchase: booty (thieves' word).   [2] would carry coals: would
do any despicable thing; carrying coal was considered one of the
most menial occupations.   [3] the disciplines of the war: military
practices.   [4] is digt himself . . . counter-mines: he has dug
counter-mines for four yards under our own mines.   [5] Cheshu:
Jesus.   [6] plow: blow.   [7] petter: better.

FLUELLEN.

It is Captain Macmorris, is it not?

GOWER.

I think it be.

FLUELLEN.

By Cheshu, he is an ass, as in the 'orld:[1] I will verify as much in his peard:[2] he has no more directions in the true disciplines of the wars, look you, of the Roman disciplines, than is a puppy-dog.

GOWER.

Here a' comes; and the Scots captain, Captain Jamy, with him.

FLUELLEN.

Captain Jamy is a marvellous falorous[3] gentleman, that is certain; and of great expedition[4] and knowledge in th'auncient wars, upon my particular knowledge of his directions: by Cheshu, he will maintain his argument as well as any military man in the 'orld, in the disciplines of the pristine[5] wars of the Romans.

Enter MACMORRIS *and* JAMY.

JAMY.

I say gude-day, Captain Fluellen.

FLUELLEN.

Got-den[6] to your worship, goot Captain Jamy.

GOWER.

How now, Captain Macmorris! have you quit the mines? have the pioners[7] given o'er?

MACMORRIS.

By Chrish, la, tish ill done; the work ish give over, the trompet sound the retreat. By my hand, I swear, and my father's soul, the work ish ill done; it ish give over: I would

---

[1] he is an ass . . . 'orld: he is as big a fool as there is in the world.   [2] I will verify . . . peard: I will say as much to his face.   [3] falorous: valorous; brave.   [4] of great expedition: has a great willingness to discuss military theory.   [5] pristine: early.   [6] Got-den: good evening.   [7] pioners: pioneers; miners (constructors of earthworks).

have blow'd up the town, so Chrish save me, la, in an hour:
O, tish ill done, tish ill done; by my hand, tish ill done!

FLUELLEN.

Captain Macmorris, I peseech[1] you now, will you voutsafe[2]
me, look you, a few disputations[3] with you, as partly touching or concerning the disciplines of the war, the Roman wars,
in the way of argument, look you, and friendly communica-
tion; partly to satisfy my opinion, and partly for the satisfaction, look you, of my mind, as touching the direction of
the military discipline; that is the point.

JAMY.

It sall be vary gude, gude feith, gude captains baith: and I
sall quit you with gude leve, as I may pick occasion; that
sall I, marry.[4]

MACMORRIS.

It is no time to discourse, so Chrish save me: the day is hot,
and the weather, and the wars, and the king, and the dukes:
it is no time to discourse. The town is beseecht,[5] and the
trompet call us to the breach; and we talk, and, be[6] Chrish,
do nothing: 'tis shame for us all: so God sa' me, 'tis shame
to stand still; it is shame, by my hand: and there is throats
to be cut, and works to be done; and there ish nothing done,
so Chrish sa' me, la.

JAMY.

By the mess,[7] ere theise eyes of mine take themselves to
slomber, ay'll de gude service, or ay'll lig[8] i'th' grund for
it; ay, or go to death; and ay'll pay't as valorously as I may,
that sall I suerly do, that is the breff and the long. Marry,
I wad full fain[9] heard some question 'tween you tway.[10]

---

[1] peseech: beseech. [2] voutsafe: vouchsafe; allow. [3] a few disputations: a few words. [4] marry: by the Virgin Mary (a mild
oath). [5] beseecht: besieged. [6] be: by. [7] mess: mass. [8] lig:
lie. [9] I wad full fain: I would gladly have. [10] tway: two.

FLUELLEN.

Captain Macmorris, I think, look you, under your correction,[1] there is not many of your nation—

MACMORRIS.

Of my nation! What ish my nation? Ish a villain, and a bastard, and a knave, and a rascal. What ish my nation? Who talks of my nation?

FLUELLEN.

Look you, if you take the matter otherwise than is meant, Captain Macmorris, peradventure I shall think you do not use me with that affability as in discretion you ought to use me, look you; being as goot a man as yourself, both in the disciplines of war, and in the derivation of my birth, and in other particularities.

MACMORRIS.

I do not know you so good a man as myself: so Chrish save me, I will cut off your head.

GOWER.

Gentlemen both, you will mistake each other.[2]

JAMY.

A! that's a foul fault.   [A parley sounded.

GOWER.

The town sounds a parley.

FLUELLEN.

Captain Macmorris, when there is more petter opportunity to be required, look you, I will be so pold as to tell you I know the disciplines of war; and there is an end.   [Exeunt.

---

[1] under your correction: correct me if I'm wrong.
[2] you will mistake each other: you are determined to misunderstand each other.

Scene III.

The same.

The GOVERNOR *and some* CITIZENS *on the walls; the English forces below. Enter* KING HENRY *and his* TRAIN *before the Gates.*

KING HENRY.

How yet resolves the governor of the town?
This is the latest parle[1] we will admit:
Therefore, to our best mercy give yourselves;
Or, like to men proud of destruction,[2]
Defy us to our worst: for, as I am a soldier,
A name that, in my thoughts, becomes me best,
If I begin the battery once again,
I will not leave the half-achieved[3] Harfleur
Till in her ashes she lie buried.
The gates of mercy shall be all shut up;
And the flesht[4] soldier,—rough and hard of heart,—
In liberty of bloody hand shall range[5]
With conscience wide as hell; mowing like grass
Your fresh-fair virgins and your flowering infants.
What is it then to me, if impious war,—
Array'd in flames, like to the prince of fiends,—
Do, with his smircht complexion, all fell feats
Enlinkt to waste and desolation? [6]
What is't to me, when you yourselves are cause,
If your pure maidens fall into the hand
Of hot and forcing violation?
What rein can hold licentious wickedness
When down the hill he holds his fierce career? [7]
We may as bootless[8] spend our vain command
Upon th'enraged soldiers in their spoil,
As send precepts[9] to the leviathan[10]
To come ashore. Therefore, you men of Harfleur
Take pity of[11] your town and of your people,

---

[1] parle: parley.　　[2] proud of destruction: elated at the thought of death.　　[3] half-achieved: half-won.　　[4] flesht: hardened by the taste of blood.　　[5] In liberty . . . range: shall pillage without restraint.　　[6] all fell feats . . . desolation: all the cruel acts associated with the sacking of cities.　　[7] fierce career: headlong charge.　　[8] bootless: vainly.　　[9] precepts: written commands.　　[10] leviathan: a huge sea monster.　　[11] of: on.

Whiles yet my soldiers are in my command;
Whiles yet the cool and temperate wind of grace[1]
O'erblows the filthy and contagious clouds
Of heady[2] murder, spoil, and villainy.
If not, why, in a moment, look to see
The blind[3] and bloody soldier with foul hand
Defile the locks of your shrill-shrieking daughters;
Your fathers taken by the silver beards,
And their most reverend heads dasht to the walls;
Your naked infants spitted upon pikes,
Whiles the mad mothers with their howls confused
Do break[4] the clouds, as did the wives of Jewry[5]
At Herod's bloody-hunting slaughtermen.[6]
What say you? will you yield, and this avoid?
Or, guilty in defence,[7] be thus destroy'd?

GOVERNOR OF HARFLEUR.

Our expectation hath this day an end:
The Dauphin, whom of succour we entreated,
Returns us,[8] that his powers are yet not ready.
To raise so great a siege. Therefore, dread king,
We yield our town and lives to thy soft mercy.
Enter our gates; dispose of us and ours;
For we no longer are defensible.

KING HENRY.

Open your gates.—Come, uncle Exeter,
Go you and enter Harfleur; there remain,
And fortify it strongly 'gainst the French:
Use mercy to them all. For us,[9] dear uncle,—
The winter coming on, and sickness growing
Upon our soldiers,—we will retire to Calais.
To-night in Harfleur will we be your guest;
To-morrow for the march are we addrest.[10]

[*Flourish, and enter the town.*

---

[1] grace: mercy.   [2] heady: headstrong; violent.   [3] blind: uncontrolled.   [4] break: pierce.   [5] Jewry: Judea.   [6] Herod's bloody-hunting slaughtermen: the Slaughter of the Innocents, Matthew 2:16.   [7] in defence: in persisting in your resistance.   [8] Returns us: sends back word to us.   [9] For us: as for us.   [10] addrest: fully prepared; ready.

Scene IV.

The French KING'S *palace.*

Enter KATHARINE *and* ALICE.

KATHARINE.

Alice, tu as été en Angleterre, et tu parles bien le langage.

ALICE.

Un peu, madame.

KATHARINE.

Je te prie m'enseignez; il faut que j'apprenne à parler. Comment appelez-vous la main en Anglois?

ALICE.

La main? elle est appelée de hand.

KATHARINE.

De hand. Et les doigts?

ALICE.

Les doigts? ma foi, j'oublie les doigts; mais je me souviendrai. Les doigts? je pense qu'ils sont appelés de fingres; *oui,* de fingres.

KATHARINE.

La main, de hand; *les doigts,* de fingres. *Je pense que je suis le bon écolier; j'ai gagné deux mots d'Anglois vitement. Comment appelez-vous les ongles?*

ALICE.

Les ongles? nous les appelons de nails.

KATHARINE.

De nails. Ecoutez; dites-moi, si je parle bien: de hand, de fingres, *et de* nails.

ALICE.

C'est bien dit, madame; il est fort bon Anglois.

In this scene, Alice teaches Katharine the English words for hand, fingers, nails, arm, elbow, neck, chin, foot. The humor of the scene lies in the fact that some of the words as Katharine pronounces them in English sound like indecent French words.

KATHARINE.

Dites-moi l'Anglois pour le bras.

ALICE.

De arm, *madame.*

KATHARINE.

Et le coude?

ALICE.

D'elbow.

KATHARINE.

D'elbow. *Je m'en fais la répétition de tous les mots que vous m'avez appris dès à présent.*

ALICE.

Il est trop difficile, madame, comme je pense.

KATHARINE.

Excusez-moi, Alice; écoutez: d'hand, de fingres, de nails, d'arm, de bilbow.

ALICE.

D'elbow, *madame.*

KATHARINE.

O Seigneur Dieu, je m'en oublie! d'elbow. *Comment appelez-vous le col?*

ALICE.

De neck, *madame.*

KATHARINE.

De nick. *Et le menton?*

ALICE.

De chin.

KATHARINE.

De sin. *Le col,* de nick; *le menton,* de sin.

ALICE.

Oui. Sauf votre honneur, en vérité, vous prononcez les mots aussi droit que les natifs d'Angleterre.

KATHARINE.

Je ne doute point d'apprendre, par la grace de Dieu, et en peu de temps.

ALICE.

N'avez-vous pas déjà oublié ce que je vous ai enseigné?

KATHARINE.

Non, je réciterai à vous promptement: d'hand, de fingres, de mails,—

ALICE.

De nails, *madame.*

KATHARINE.

De nails, de arm, de ilbow.

ALICE.

Sauf votre honneur, d'elbow.

KATHARINE.

Ainsi dis-je; d'elbow, de nick, *et* de sin. *Comment appelez-vous le pied et la robe?*

ALICE.

De foot, *madame; et* de coun.

KATHARINE.

De foot *et* de coun! *O Seigneur Dieu! ce sont mots de son mauvais, corruptible, gros, et impudique, et non pour les dames d'honneur d'user: je ne voudrais prononcer ces mots devant les seigneurs de France pour tout le monde. Foh! le* foot *et le* coun! *Néanmoins, je réciterai une autre fois ma leçon ensemble:* d'hand, de fingres, de nails, d'arm, d'elbow, de nick, de sin, de foot, de coun.

ALICE.

Excellent madame!

KATHARINE.

C'est assez pour une fois: allons-nous à diner. [*Exeunt.*

Scene V.

The same.

Enter the KING OF FRANCE, *the* DAUPHIN, BOURBON, *the* CONSTABLE OF FRANCE, *and others.*

FRENCH KING.

'Tis certain he hath past the river Somme.

THE CONSTABLE OF FRANCE.

And if he be not fought withal, my lord,
Let us not live in France; let us quit all,
And give our vineyards to a barbarous people.

DAUPHIN.

O Dieu vivant! [1] shall a few sprays of us, [2]
The emptying of our fathers' luxury, [3]
Our scions, put in wild and savage [4] stock,
Spirt [5] up so suddenly into the clouds,
And overlook [6] their grafters?

DUKE OF BOURBON.

Normans, but bastard Normans, Norman bastards!
Mort de ma vie! [7] if they march along
Unfought withal, but I will [8] sell my dukedom,
To buy a slobbery [9] and a dirty farm
In that nook-shotten isle of Albion. [10]

THE CONSTABLE OF FRANCE.

Dieu de batailles! [11] where have they this mettle? [12]
Is not their climate foggy, raw, and dull;
On whom, as in despite, the sun looks pale,
Killing their fruit with frowns? Can sodden water,
A drench for sur-rein'd jades, [13] their barley-broth, [14]

---

[1] *Dieu vivant:* by the living God.   [2] a few sprays of us: a reference to the Norman-French blood in some of the English.   [3] luxury: lust.   [4] savage: uncultivated.   [5] Spirt: spurt.   [6] overlook: look down on.   [7] *Mort de ma vie:* death of my life.   [8] but I will: if I will not.   [9] slobbery: muddy; foul.   [10] nook-shotten isle of Albion: inaccessible corner of the globe (England).   [11] *Dieu de batailles:* god of battles.   [12] mettle: courage.   [13] surrein'd jades: overridden nags.   [14] barley-broth: ale (used in treating horses).

Decoct[1] their cold blood to such valiant heat?
And shall our quick blood, spirited with wine,
Seem frosty? O, for honour of our land,
Let us not hang like roping[2] icicles
Upon our houses' thatch, whiles a more frosty people
Sweat drops of gallant youth in our rich fields,—
Poor we may call them in their native lords! [3]

    DAUPHIN.

By faith and honour,
Our madams mock at us, and plainly say
Our mettle is bred out, and they will give
Their bodies to the lust of English youth
To new-store France with bastard warriors.

    DUKE OF BOURBON.

They bid us to the English dancing-schools,
And[4] teach lavoltas[5] high and swift corantos;[6]
Saying our grace[7] is only in our heels,
And that we are most lofty runaways.[8]

    FRENCH KING.

Where is Montjoy the herald? speed him hence;
Let him greet England with our sharp defiance.—
Up, princes! and, with spirit of honour edged
More sharper than your swords, hie[9] to the field:
Charles Delabreth, high-Constable of France;
You Dukes of Orleans, Bourbon, and of Berri,
Alençon, Brabant, Bar, and Burgundy;
Jaques Chatillon, Rambures, Vaudemont,
Beaumont, Grandpré, Roussi, and Fauconberg,
Foix, Lestrale, Bouciqualt, and Charolois;
High dukes, great princes, barons, lords, and knights,
For your great seats[10] now quit you[11] of great shames.
Bar Harry England, that sweeps through our land

---

[1] Decoct: warm; heat up.   [2] roping: dangling.   [3] Poor . . .
lords: that is, the lands are poor because of their worthless owners.
[4] And: to.   [5] lavoltas: leaping dances.   [6] corantos: a dance with
quick-gliding or running steps.   [7] grace: virtue; worth.   [8] lofty
runaways: high-stepping cowards (renegades).   [9] hie: hasten.
[10] seats: estates; holdings.   [11] quit you: rid yourselves.

With pennons painted in the blood of Harfleur:
Rush on his host, as doth the melted snow
Upon the valleys, whose low vassal seat
The Alps doth spit and void his rheum[1] upon:
Go down upon him,—you have power enough,—
And in a captive chariot into Rouen
Bring him our prisoner.

THE CONSTABLE OF FRANCE.

                     This becomes the great.
Sorry am I his numbers are so few,
His soldiers sick, and famisht in their march;
For I am sure, when he shall see our army,
He'll drop his heart into the sink of fear,
And for achievement[2] offer us his ransom.

FRENCH KING.

Therefore, lord Constable, haste on Montjoy;
And let him say to England, that we send
To know what willing ransom he will give.—
Prince Dauphin, you shall stay with us in Rouen.

DAUPHIN.

Not so, I do beseech your majesty.

FRENCH KING.

Be patient; for you shall remain with us.
Now forth, lord Constable, and princes all,
And quickly bring us word of England's fall.   [Exeunt.

Scene VI.

The English camp in Picardy.

Enter GOWER *and* FLUELLEN, *meeting.*

GOWER.

How now, Captain Fluellen! come you from the bridge?

---

[1] void his rheum: spit its phlegm.
[2] for achievement: instead of fighting.

FLUELLEN.

I assure you, there is very excellent services committed at the
pridge.

GOWER.

Is the Duke of Exeter safe?

FLUELLEN.

The Duke of Exeter is as magnanimous[1] as Agamemnon;[2]
and a man that I love and honour with my soul, and my
heart, and my duty, and my life, and my living, and my
uttermost power: he is not—Got be praised and plest!—
any hurt in the 'orld; but keeps the pridge most valiantly,
with excellent discipline. There is an auncient[3] there at
the pridge,—I think in my very conscience he is as valiant
a man as Mark Antony; and he is a man of no estimation[4]
in the 'orld; but I did see him do gallant service.

GOWER.

What do you call him?

FLUELLEN.

He is called Auncient Pistol.

GOWER.

I know him not.

FLUELLEN.

Here is the man.

Enter PISTOL.

PISTOL.

Captain, I thee beseech to do me favours:
The Duke of Exeter doth love thee well.

FLUELLEN.

Ay, I praise Got; and I have merited some love at his hands.

---

[1] magnanimous: of great courage.
[2] Agamemnon: general of the Greek forces that attacked Troy.
[3] auncient: ancient; ensign.
[4] estimation: reputation.

PISTOL.

Bardolph, a soldier, firm and sound of heart,
And of buxom[1] valour, hath, by cruel fate,
And giddy Fortune's furious fickle wheel,—
That goddess blind,
That stands upon the rolling restless stone,—

FLUELLEN.

By your patience, Auncient Pistol. Fortune is painted plind,
with a muffler afore her eyes, to signify to you that Fortune
is plind; and she is painted also with a wheel, to signify
to you, which is the moral of it, that she is turning, and
inconstant, and mutability, and variation: and her foot, look
you, is fixt upon a spherical stone, which rolls, and rolls,
and rolls:—in good truth, the poet makes a most excellent
description of it: Fortune is an excellent moral.

PISTOL.

Fortune is Bardolph's foe, and frowns on him;
For he hath stoln a pax,[2] and hanged must a' be,—
A damned death!
Let gallows gape for dog; let man go free,
And let not hemp his windpipe suffocate:[3]
But Exeter hath given the doom of death
For pax of little price.
Therefore, go speak,—the duke will hear thy voice;
And let not Bardolph's vital thread be cut
With edge of penny cord and vile reproach:
Speak, captain, for his life, and I will thee requite.[4]

FLUELLEN.

Auncient Pistol, I partly understand your meaning.

---

[1] buxom: lively.
[2] a pax: in Holinshed's account, the word is *pyx;* a *pyx* or *pix* is a
box of consecrated wafers; a *pax* is the stamped figure of a crucifix,
which is kissed by the priest and then by the worshipper.
[3] let not hemp his windpipe suffocate: let him not be hanged.
[4] requite: repay.

PISTOL.

Why, then, rejoice therefore.

FLUELLEN.

Certainly, auncient, it is not a thing to rejoice at: for if, look you, he were my prother, I would desire the duke to use his goot pleasure, and put him to execution; for discipline ought to be used.

PISTOL.

Die and be damn'd! and figo[1] for thy friendship!

FLUELLEN.

It is well.

PISTOL.

The fig of Spain!   [*Exit.*

FLUELLEN.

Very goot.

GOWER.

Why, this is an arrant[2] counterfeit rascal; I remember him now; a bawd, a cutpurse.[3]

FLUELLEN.

I'll assure you, a' utter'd as prave 'ords at the pridge as you shall see in a summer's day. But it is very well; what he has spoke to me, that is well, I warrant you, when time is serve.[4]

GOWER.

Why, 'tis a gull, a fool, a rogue, that now and then goes to the wars, to grace himself, at his return into London, under the form of a soldier. And such fellows are perfect[5] in the great commanders' names: and they will learn you by rote[6] where services were done;—at such and such a sconce,[7] at

---

[1] figo: Spanish for fig, a word often used contemptuously. [2] arrant: outright. [3] cutpurse: pickpocket. [4] when time is serve: that is, he will be revenged at the first opportunity. [5] perfect: letter perfect. [6] learn you by rote: memorize. [7] sconce: bulwark; earthwork.

such a breach, at such a convoy; who came off bravely, who was shot, who disgraced, what terms the enemy stood on; and this they con[1] perfectly in the phrase of war, which they trick up with new-turn'd oaths: and what a beard of the general's cut,[2] and a horrid suit of the camp, will do among foaming bottles and ale-washt wits, is wonderful to be thought on. But you must learn to know such slanders of the age,[3] or else you may be marvellously mistook.

FLUELLEN.

I tell you what, Captain Gower;—I do perceive he is not the man that he would gladly make show to the 'orld he is: if I find a hole in his coat, I will tell him my mind. [*Drum within.*] Hark you, the king is coming; and I must speak with him from the pridge.[4]

Drum and colours. Enter KING HENRY, GLOSTER, *and his poor*
                          SOLDIERS.

Got pless your majesty!

KING HENRY.

How now, Fluellen! camest thou from the bridge?

FLUELLEN.

Ay, so please your majesty. The Duke of Exeter has very gallantly maintain'd the pridge: the French is gone off, look you; and there is gallant and most prave passages:[5] marry, th'athversary[6] was have[7] possession of the pridge; but he is enforced[8] to retire, and the Duke of Exeter is master of the pridge: I can tell your majesty, the duke is a prave man.

KING HENRY.

What men have you lost, Fluellen?

---

[1] con: know; learn by heart.   [2] what a beard of the general's cut: which general wears his beard in a certain way.   [3] Slanders of the age: disgracers or abusers of our time.   [4] from the pridge: about the bridge.   [5] passages: actions.   [6] athversary: adversary.   [7] was have: had.   [8] enforced: forced.

FLUELLEN.

The perdition[1] of th'athversary hath been very great, reasonable great: marry, for my part, I think the duke hath lost never a man, but one that is like to be executed for robbing a church,—one Bardolph, if your majesty know the man: his face is all bubukles,[2] and whelks,[3] and knobs, and flames o' fire: and his lips plows at his nose, and it is like a coal of fire, sometimes plue and sometimes red; but his nose is executed,[4] and his fire's out.

KING HENRY.

We would have all such offenders so cut off, and we give express charge that in our marches through the country, there be nothing compelled[5] from the villages, nothing taken but paid for, none of the French upbraided or abused in disdainful language; for when lenity and cruelty play for a kingdom, the gentler gamester is the soonest winner.

Tucket.[6] *Enter* MONTJOY.

MONTJOY.

You know me by my habit.[7]

KING HENRY.

Well, then, I know thee: what shall I know of thee? [8]

MONTJOY.

My master's mind.

KING HENRY.

Unfold it.

MONTJOY.

Thus says my king:—Say thou to Harry of England: Though we seem'd dead, we did but sleep; advantage[9] is a better soldier than rashness. Tell him, we could have rebuked him at

---

[1] perdition: loss of life.   [2] bubukles: Fluellen combines "bubo" and "carbuncle" to coin this word.   [3] whelks: red pimples.   [4] executed: slit (before being hanged).   [5] compelled: taken by force.   [6] *Tucket:* the sound of a trumpet.   [7] habit: herald's coat.   [8] of thee: from you.   [9] advantage: waiting for the most favorable opportunity.

Harfleur, but that we thought not good to bruise an injury
till it were full ripe:—[1] now we speak upon our cue,[2] and
our voice is imperial: England shall repent his folly, see his
weakness, and admire our sufferance.[3] Bid him, therefore,
consider of his ransom; which must proportion[4] the losses we
have borne, the subjects we have lost, the disgrace we have
digested; which, in weight to reanswer, his pettiness[5] would
bow under. For our losses, his exchequer is too poor; for
th'effusion of our blood, the muster of his kingdom too faint
a number; and for our disgrace, his own person, kneeling at
our feet, but a weak and worthless satisfaction. To this add
defiance: and tell him, for conclusion, he hath betray'd his
followers, whose condemnation is pronounced. So far my king
and master; so much my office.

    KING HENRY.

What is thy name? I know thy quality.[6]

    MONTJOY.

Montjoy.

    KING HENRY.

Thou dost thy office fairly. Turn thee back,
And tell thy king,—I do not seek him now;
But could be willing to march on to Calais
Without impeachment:[7] for, to say the sooth,—[8]
Though 'tis no wisdom to confess so much
Unto an enemy of craft and vantage,—[9]
My people are with sickness much enfeebled;
My numbers lessen'd; and those few I have,
Almost no better than so many French;
Who when they were in health, I tell thee, herald,

---

[1] to bruise . . . ripe: an allusion to the practice of waiting for a
carbuncle to be ripe before lancing it.   [2] upon our cue: at the
proper moment.   [3] admire our sufferance: wonder at our for-
bearance.   [4] proportion: be in proportion to.   [5] his pettiness: a
man so weak.   [6] quality: profession.   [7] impeachment: hindrance.
[8] sooth: truth.   [9] of craft and vantage: who is not only clever, but
also has the advantage.

I thought upon one pair of English legs
Did march three Frenchmen.—Yet, forgive me, God,
That I do brag thus!—this your air of France
Hath blown[1] that vice in me; I must repent.
Go, therefore, tell thy master here I am;
My ransom is this frail and worthless trunk;[2]
My army but a weak and sickly guard:
Yet, God before,[3] tell him we will come on,
Though France himself, and such another neighbour,
Stand in our way. There's for thy labour, Montjoy.

                              [*Gives a purse.*

Go, bid thy master well advise himself:[4]
If we may pass, we will; if we be hinder'd,
We shall your tawny[5] ground with your red blood
Discolour: and so, Montjoy, fare you well.
The sum of all our answer is but this:
We would not seek a battle, as we are;
Nor, as we are, we say, we will not shun it:
So tell your master.

      MONTJOY.

I shall deliver so.[6] Thanks to your highness.   [*Exit.*

      DUKE OF GLOSTER.

I hope they will not come upon us now.

      KING HENRY.

We are in God's hand, brother, not in theirs.
March to the bridge; it now draws toward night:—
Beyond the river we'll encamp ourselves;
And on to-morrow bid them march away.   [*Exeunt.*

---

[1] blown: encouraged; inflated.

[2] trunk: body.

[3] God before: with God leading us.

[4] well advise himself: to think carefully.

[5] tawny: yellow.

[6] so: as you have said.

Scene VII.

The French camp near Agincourt.

Enter the CONSTABLE OF FRANCE, *the* LORD RAMBURES, ORLEANS, *the* DAUPHIN, *and others.*

THE CONSTABLE OF FRANCE.

Tut! I have the best armour[1] of the world.—Would it were day!

DUKE OF ORLEANS.

You have an excellent armour; but let my horse have his due.

THE CONSTABLE OF FRANCE.

It is the best horse of Europe.

DUKE OF ORLEANS.

Will it never be morning?

DAUPHIN.

My Lord of Orleans, and my lord high-Constable, you talk of horse and armour?

DUKE OF ORLEANS.

You are as well provided of both as any prince in the world.

DAUPHIN.

What a long night is this!—I will not change[2] my horse with any that treads but on four pasterns.[3] *Ça, ha!* he bounds from the earth, as if his entrails were hairs;[4] *le cheval volant,* the Pegasus,[5] *qui a les narines de feu!* When I bestride him, I soar, I am a hawk: he trots the air; the earth sings when he touches it; the basest horn of his hoof is more musical than the pipe of Hermes.[6]

DUKE OF ORLEANS.

He's of the colour of the nutmeg.

---

[1] armour: suit of armor.   [2] change: trade.   [3] pasterns: that part of a horse's foot between the hoof and the fetlock.   [4] as if his entrails were hairs: as if he were stuffed with hair (as a tennis ball).   [5] Pegasus: the winged horse of Bellerophon.   [6] the pipe of Hermes: the shepherd's pipe (syrinx) invented by Hermes (Mercury).

DAUPHIN.

And of the heat of the ginger. It is a beast for Perseus:[1] he is pure air and fire; and the dull elements of earth and water never appear in him, but only in patient stillness while his rider mounts him: he is, indeed, a horse; and all other jades you may call beasts.

THE CONSTABLE OF FRANCE.

Indeed, my lord, it is a most absolute[2] and excellent horse.

DAUPHIN.

It is the prince of palfreys; his neigh is like the bidding of a monarch, and his countenance enforces homage.

DUKE OF ORLEANS.

No more, cousin.

DAUPHIN.

Nay, the man hath no wit that cannot, from the rising of the lark to the lodging[3] of the lamb, vary deserved praise on my palfrey:[4] it is a theme as fluent as the sea; turn the sands into eloquent tongues, and my horse is argument[5] for them all: 'tis a subject for a sovereign to reason on, and for a sovereign's sovereign to ride on; and for the world, familiar to us and unknown,[6] to lay apart their particular functions, and wonder at him. I once writ a sonnet in his praise, and began thus: 'Wonder of nature,'—

DUKE OF ORLEANS.

I have heard a sonnet begin so to one's mistress.

DAUPHIN.

Then did they imitate that which I composed to my courser; for my horse is my mistress.

---

[1] Perseus: Mercury lent Perseus his winged shoes.   [2] absolute: perfect.   [3] lodging: lying down.   [4] palfrey: saddle horse.   [5] argument: a worthy subject.   [6] familiar to us and unknown: that is, whether familiar to us or unknown.

DUKE OF ORLEANS.

Your mistress bears well.

DAUPHIN.

Me well; which is the prescript[1] praise and perfection of a good and particular mistress.

THE CONSTABLE OF FRANCE.

Ma foi, methought yesterday your mistress shrewdly[2] shook your back.

DAUPHIN.

So, perhaps, did yours.

THE CONSTABLE OF FRANCE.

Mine was not bridled.

DAUPHIN.

O, then, belike[3] she was old and gentle; and you rode, like a kern of Ireland,[4] your French hose[5] off, and in your strait strossers.[6]

THE CONSTABLE OF FRANCE.

You have good judgement in horsemanship.

DAUPHIN.

Be warn'd by me, then: they that ride so, and ride not warily, fall into foul bogs. I had rather have my horse to my mistress.

THE CONSTABLE OF FRANCE.

I had as lief have my mistress a jade.[7]

DAUPHIN.

I tell thee, constable, my mistress wears her own hair.[8]

THE CONSTABLE OF FRANCE.

I could make as true a boast as that, if I had a sow to my mistress.

DAUPHIN.

Le chien est retourné à son propre vomissement, et la truie lavée au bourbier:[9] thou makest use of any thing.

---

[1] prescript: normal; prescribed.   [2] shrewdly: mischievously; ill-humoredly.   [3] belike: most likely.   [4] kern of Ireland: rough Irish foot soldier.   [5] French hose: baggy trousers.   [6] strait strossers: skimpy trousers.   [7] jade: a worthless horse or woman.   [8] wears her own hair: an allusion to the custom of wearing wigs.   [9] *Le chien . . . bourbier:* from II Peter 2:22—"The dog *is* turned to his own vomit again; and, The sow that was washed to her wallowing in the mire."

THE CONSTABLE OF FRANCE.

Yet do I not use my horse for my mistress; or any such proverb, so little kin to the purpose.

RAMBURES.

My lord constable, the armour that I saw in your tent to-night, —are those stars or suns upon it?

THE CONSTABLE OF FRANCE.

Stars, my lord.

DAUPHIN.

Some of them will fall to-morrow, I hope.

THE CONSTABLE OF FRANCE.

And yet my sky shall not want.

DAUPHIN.

That may be, for you bear a many superfluously, and 'twere more honour some were away.

THE CONSTABLE OF FRANCE.

Even as your horse bears your praises; who would trot as well, were some of your brags dismounted.[1]

DAUPHIN.

Would I were able to load him with his desert!—Will it never be day?—I will trot to-morrow a mile, and my way shall be paved with English faces.

THE CONSTABLE OF FRANCE.

I will not say so, for fear I should be faced out of my way:[2] but I would it were morning; for I would fain be about the ears of the English.

RAMBURES.

Who will go to hazard[3] with me for twenty prisoners?

THE CONSTABLE OF FRANCE.

You must first go yourself to hazard, ere[4] you have them.

---

[1] dismounted: cut down a peg.
[2] be faced out of my way: be put to shame; lose face.
[3] go to hazard: wager; play craps.
[4] ere: before.

DAUPHIN.

'Tis midnight; I'll go arm myself.   [*Exit.*

DUKE OF ORLEANS.

The Dauphin longs for morning.

RAMBURES.

He longs to eat the English.

THE CONSTABLE OF FRANCE.

I think he will eat all he kills.

DUKE OF ORLEANS.

By the white hand of my lady, he's a gallant prince.

THE CONSTABLE OF FRANCE.

Swear by her foot, that she may tread out the oath.

DUKE OF ORLEANS.

He is, simply, the most active gentleman of France.

THE CONSTABLE OF FRANCE.

Doing is activity:[1] and he will still be doing.[2]

DUKE OF ORLEANS.

He never did harm, that I heard of.

THE CONSTABLE OF FRANCE.

Nor will do none to-morrow: he will keep that good name still.

DUKE OF ORLEANS.

I know him to be valiant.

THE CONSTABLE OF FRANCE.

I was told that by one that knows him better than you.

DUKE OF ORLEANS.

What's he?

THE CONSTABLE OF FRANCE.

Marry, he told me so himself; and he said he cared not who knew it.

---

[1] Doing is activity: that is, playing the fool.
[2] still be doing: always be doing it.

DUKE OF ORLEANS.

He needs not; it is no hidden virtue in him.

THE CONSTABLE OF FRANCE.

By my faith, sir, but it is; never any body saw it but his lackey:[1] 'tis a hooded valour; and when it appears, it will bate.[2]

DUKE OF ORLEANS.

Ill-will never said well.

THE CONSTABLE OF FRANCE.

I will cap[3] that proverb with—There is flattery in friendship.

DUKE OF ORLEANS.

And I will take up that with—Give the devil his due.

THE CONSTABLE OF FRANCE.

Well placed:[4] there stands your friend for the devil: have at the very eye of that proverb, with—A pox of the devil.

DUKE OF ORLEANS.

You are the better by proverbs, by how much—A fool's bolt[5] is soon shot.

THE CONSTABLE OF FRANCE.

You have shot over.[6]

DUKE OF ORLEANS.

'Tis not the first time you were overshot.[7]

Enter a MESSENGER.

MESSENGER.

My lord high-Constable, the English lie within fifteen hundred paces of your tents.

THE CONSTABLE OF FRANCE.

Who hath measured the ground?

MESSSENGER.

The Lord Grandpré.

---

[1] never . . . lackey: "He has beaten nobody but his footboy"—Johnson.   [2] 'tis a hooded valour . . . bate: his courage is hidden most of the time (as a falcon is hooded), but when he shows it, it will soon abate (with a pun on bait—the flapping of the falcon's wings when it is uncovered).   [3] cap: top.   [4] Well placed: well said.   [5] bolt: a blunt-headed arrow.   [6] shot over: overshot the mark (target).   [7] overshot: outshot.

THE CONSTABLE OF FRANCE.

A valiant and most expert gentleman.—Would it were day!—
Alas, poor Harry of England! he longs not for the dawning, as
we do.

DUKE OF ORLEANS.

What a wretched and peevish[1] fellow is this King of England,
to mope with his fat-brain'd [2] followers so far out of his knowledge!

THE CONSTABLE OF FRANCE.

If the English had any apprehension,[3] they would run away.

DUKE OF ORLEANS.

That they lack; for if their heads had any intellectual armour,
they could never wear such heavy head-pieces.

RAMBURES.

That island of England breeds very valiant creatures; their
mastiffs[4] are of unmatchable courage.

DUKE OF ORLEANS.

Foolish curs, that run winking[5] into the mouth of a Russian
bear, and have their heads crusht like rotten apples! You may
as well say, that's a valiant flea that dare eat his breakfast on
the lip of a lion.

THE CONSTABLE OF FRANCE.

Just, just; and the men do sympathize[6] with the mastiffs in
robustious[7] and rough coming-on, leaving their wits with their
wives: and then give them great meals of beef, and iron and
steel, they will eat like wolves, and fight like devils.

DUKE OF ORLEANS.

Ay, but these English are shrewdly[8] out of beef.

---

[1] peevish: silly; childish.   [2] fat-brain'd: dull; fatheaded.   [3] had
any apprehension: were intelligent enough to know the meaning of
fear.   [4] mastiffs: English dogs used in bear-baiting.   [5] winking:
blindly (with their eyes shut).   [6] do sympathize: as in accord.
[7] robustious: violent.   [8] shrewdly: badly; grievously.

THE CONSTABLE OF FRANCE.

Then shall we find to-morrow they have only stomachs to eat,
and none to fight. Now is it time to arm; come, shall we about
it?

DUKE OF ORLEANS.

It is now two o'clock: but, let me see,—by ten
We shall have each a hundred Englishmen.   [*Exeunt.*

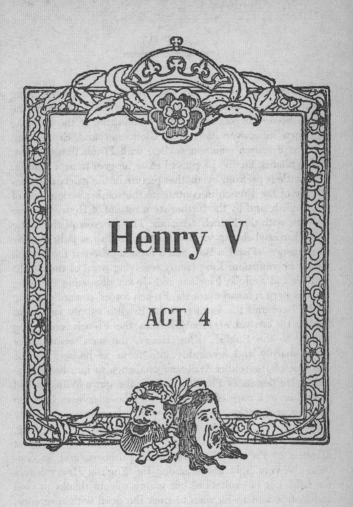

Henry V

ACT 4

ACT IV

THE PROLOGUE centers on the "royal captain," the King moving as a man among his forces during the night before the battle. Scene i makes explicit the humanizing of the king: he is shown in conversation with Gloucester and Erpingham; then, as if only a common soldier, with Pistol, Bates, Court, and Williams; finally, he prays before he goes to arm himself. The battle is prefixed by another picture of the gaiety and confidence of the French in contrast to the somber seriousness of the English, and by the further stern refusal of Henry to come to terms with the French demands. The progress of the battle toward overwhelming victory for the English is indicated by short scenes—Pistol, a Boy, and a French prisoner; the French nobles in confusion; King Henry receiving word of the deaths of York and Suffolk; Fluellen and Gower discussing the King and his stern retaliation for the French forces' cowardly killing of the boys and the looting of the English supply vans; and finally, the arrival of Montjoy from the French, conceding victory to the English. King Henry, the *man*, comes once again sharply and admirably into focus as he sees to the outcome of the soldier Williams' challenge to him before the battle. He deputizes Fluellen to wear the glove Williams had given him as a gage of challenge; then he intervenes between the two and settles the dispute with a handsome reward to Williams, who had seen, talked to, and challenged the king, "but as a common man." Finally, with word of the great numbers of French killed and taken prisoners, and, in contrast, the very light losses among the English, Henry leaves the field, not in exultation, but giving solemn thanks to God and instructions to his men to treat the dead with reverence.

ACT IV. PROLOGUE.

Enter CHORUS.

CHORUS.

Now entertain conjecture of[1] a time
When creeping murmur and the poring[2] dark
Fills the wide vessel of the universe.
From camp to camp, through the foul womb of night,
The hum of either army stilly sounds,[3]
That[4] the fixt sentinels almost receive
The secret whispers of each other's watch:
Fire answers fire; and through their paly flames
Each battle[5] sees the other's umber'd[6] face:
Steed threatens steed, in high and boastful neighs
Piercing the night's dull ear; and from the tents,
The armourers, accomplishing[7] the knights,
With busy hammers closing rivets up,
Give dreadful note of preparation:
The country cocks do crow, the clocks do toll,
And the third hour of drowsy morning name.
Proud of their numbers, and secure in soul,[8]
The confident and over-lusty[9] French
Do the low-rated English play[10] at dice;

---

[1] entertain conjecture of: imagine.   [2] poring: peering; "straining
the eyes and yet seeing only the nearest things, purblind"—
Schmidt.   [3] stilly sounds: comes clearly through the quiet night.
[4] That: so that.   [5] battle: army.   [6] umber'd: darkly colored by
firelight.   [7] accomplishing: finishing the armor of.   [8] secure in
soul: overconfident, and, therefore, careless.   [9] over-lusty: too
merry.   [10] play: play for.

And chide the cripple tardy-gaited[1] night,
Who, like a foul and ugly witch, doth limp
So tediously away. The poor condemned English,
Like sacrifices, by their watchful fires
Sit patiently, and inly[2] ruminate
The morning's danger; and their gesture sad[3]
Investing lank-lean cheeks, and war-worn coats,
Presenteth them unto the gazing moon
So many horrid ghosts. O, now, who will behold
The royal captain of this ruin'd band
Walking from watch to watch, from tent to tent,
Let him cry, 'Praise and glory on his head!'
For forth he goes and visits all his host;
Bids them good morrow with a modest smile,
And calls them brothers, friends, and countrymen.
Upon his royal face there is no note
How dread an army hath enrounded[4] him;
Nor doth he dedicate one jot of colour
Unto the weary and all-watched night:[5]
But freshly looks, and over-bears attaint[6]
With cheerful semblance and sweet majesty;
That every wretch, pining and pale before,
Beholding him, plucks comfort from his looks:
A largess universal,[7] like the sun,
His liberal eye doth give to every one,
Thawing cold fear. Then, mean and gentle all,[8]
Behold, as may unworthiness[9] define,
A little touch of Harry in the night:
And so our scene must to the battle fly;
Where—O for pity!—we shall much disgrace
With four or five most vile and ragged foils,[10]
Right ill-disposed, in brawl ridiculous,

---

[1] tardy-gaited: slow-moving.   [2] inly: inwardly.   [3] gesture sad: serious mien.   [4] enrounded: surrounded.   [5] dedicate . . . night: lose any of his rosy color because of the wearing and wakeful night.   [6] over-bears attaint: overcomes all signs of exhaustion.   [7] A largess universal: that is, his generosity is extended to everyone.   [8] mean and gentle all: all ranks of men.   [9] unworthiness: this unworthy one.   [10] foils: swordsmen.

The name of Agincourt. Yet, sit and see;
Minding[1] true things by what their mockeries[2] be.

[*Exit.*

Scene I.

The English camp at Agincourt.

Enter KING HENRY, BEDFORD, *and* GLOSTER.

KING HENRY.

Gloster, 'tis true that we are in great danger;
The greater therefore should our courage be.—
Good morrow, brother Bedford.—God Almighty!
There is some soul[3] of goodness in things evil,
Would men observingly distil it out;
For our bad neighbour makes us early stirrers,
Which is both healthful and good husbandry:[4]
Besides, they are our outward consciences,
And preachers to us all; admonishing
That we should dress us[5] fairly for our end.
Thus may we gather honey from the weed,
And make a moral of[6] the devil himself.

Enter ERPINGHAM.

Good morrow, old Sir Thomas Erpingham:
A good soft pillow for that good white head
Were better than a churlish[7] turf of France.

SIR THOMAS ERPINGHAM.

Not so, my liege: this lodging likes me[8] better,
Since I may say, 'Now lie I like a king.'

KING HENRY.

'Tis good for men to love their present pains
Upon[9] example; so the spirit is eased:

---

[1] Minding: calling to mind; bearing in mind.   [2] mockeries: poor
imitations.   [3] soul: core.   [4] husbandry: thrift.   [5] dress us: prepare ourselves.   [6] make . . . of: find a moral lesson in.
[7] churlish: rough.   [8] likes me: pleases me.   [9] Upon: because of.

And when the mind is quicken'd, out of doubt[1]
The organs, though defunct[2] and dead before,
Break up their drowsy grave, and newly move
With casted slough[3] and fresh legerity.[4]
Lend me thy cloak, Sir Thomas.—Brothers both,
Commend me to the princes in our camp;
Do[5] my good morrow to them; and anon
Desire them all to my pavilion.

DUKE OF GLOSTER.

We shall, my liege.

SIR THOMAS ERPINGHAM.

Shall I attend your Grace?

KING HENRY.

                    No, my good knight;
Go with my brothers to my lords of England:
I and my bosom[6] must debate awhile,
And then I would no other company.

SIR THOMAS ERPINGHAM.

The Lord in heaven bless thee, noble Harry!

[*Exeunt* GLOSTER, BEDFORD, *and* ERPINGHAM.

KING HENRY.

God-a-mercy,[7] old heart! thou speak'st cheerfully.

Enter PISTOL.

PISTOL.

Qui va là? [8]

KING HENRY.

A friend.

PISTOL.

Discuss[9] unto me; art thou officer?
Or art thou base, common, and popular?

KING HENRY.

I am a gentleman of a company.

---

[1] out of doubt: without doubt.   [2] defunct: useless.   [3] casted
slough: cast-off skin (as a snake sheds its skin).   [4] legerity:
lightness.   [5] Do: give.   [6] bosom: secret thoughts.   [7] God-a-
mercy: a corruption of God have mercy; thank you.   [8] *Qui va
là*: who goes there.   [9] Discuss: reveal yourself.

PISTOL.

Trail'st thou the puissant pike? [1]

KING HENRY.

Even so. What are you?

PISTOL.

As good a gentleman as the emperor.

KING HENRY.

Then you are a better than the king.

PISTOL.

The king's a bawcock,[2] and a heart of gold,
A lad of life, an imp[3] of fame;
Of parents good, of fist most valiant:
I kiss his dirty shoe, and from heart-string
I love the lovely bully.—What is thy name?

KING HENRY.

Harry *le Roy*.

PISTOL.

Le Roy!
A Cornish name: art thou of Cornish crew?

KING HENRY.

No, I am a Welshman.

PISTOL.

Know'st thou Fluellen?

KING HENRY.

Yes.

PISTOL.

Tell him, I'll knock his leek about his pate
Upon Saint Davy's day.[4]

KING HENRY.

Do not you wear your dagger in your cap that day, lest he
knock that about yours.

PISTOL.

Art thou his friend?

---

[1] Trail'st . . . pike: that is, are you a member of the infantry.
[2] bawcock: *beau coq;* fine fellow.
[3] imp: youth.
[4] Saint Davy's day: Saint David's day—the 1st of March, and the
anniversary of the victory of the Welsh (wearers of the leek) over
the Saxons.

KING HENRY.

And his kinsman too.

PISTOL.

The figo[1] for thee, then!

KING HENRY.

I thank you: God be with you!

PISTOL.

My name is Pistol call'd.   [*Exit.*

KING HENRY.

It sorts[2] well with your fierceness.

Enter FLUELLEN *and* GOWER, *severally.*

GOWER.

Captain Fluellen!

FLUELLEN.

So! in the name of Cheshu Christ, speak lower. It is the greatest admiration[3] in the universal 'orld, when the true and auncient prerogatifs and laws of the wars is not kept: if you would take the pains but to examine the wars of Pompey the Great, you shall find, I warrant you, that there is no tiddle-taddle nor pibble-pabble in Pompey's camp; I warrant you, you shall find the ceremonies of the wars, and the cares of it, and the forms of it, and the sobriety of it, and the modesty[4] of it, to be otherwise.

GOWER.

Why, the enemy is loud; you heard him all night.

FLUELLEN.

If the enemy is an ass, and a fool, and a prating coxcomb, is it meet, think you, that we should also, look you, be an ass, and a fool, and a prating coxcomb,—in your own conscience, now?

---

[1] figo: fig (a derisive term).

[2] sorts: agrees.

[3] admiration: marvel; wonder.

[4] modesty: moderation.

GOWER.

I will speak lower.

FLUELLEN.

I pray you, and peseech you, that you will.

[*Exeunt* GOWER *and* FLUELLEN.

KING HENRY.

Though it appear a little out of fashion,[1]
There is much care and valour in this Welshman.

Enter three SOLDIERS, JOHN BATES, ALEXANDER COURT, *and*
MICHAEL WILLIAMS.

ALEXANDER COURT.

Brother John Bates, is not that the morning which breaks
yonder?

JOHN BATES.

I think it be: but we have no great cause to desire the approach of day.

MICHAEL WILLIAMS.

We see yonder the beginning of the day, but I think we shall
never see the end of it.—Who goes there?

KING HENRY.

A friend.

MICHAEL WILLIAMS.

Under what captain serve you?

KING HENRY.

Under Sir Thomas Erpingham.

MICHAEL WILLIAMS.

A good old commander and a most kind gentleman: I pray
you, what thinks he of our estate? [2]

KING HENRY.

Even as men wrackt[3] upon a sand, that look to be washt off
the next tide.

JOHN BATES.

He hath not told his thought to the king?

---

[1] out of fashion: eccentric.
[2] estate: condition; state.
[3] wrackt: wrecked.

KING HENRY.

No; nor it is meet[1] he should. For, though I speak it to you, I think the king is but a man, as I am: the violet smells to him as it doth to me; the element[2] shows[3] to him as it doth to me; all his senses have but human conditions:[4] his ceremonies[5] laid by, in his nakedness he appears but a man; and though his affections are higher mounted than ours, yet, when they stoop,[6] they stoop with the like wing. Therefore when he sees reason of fears, as we do, his fears, out of doubt,[7] be of the same relish as ours are: yet, in reason, no man should possess him with any appearance of fear,[8] lest he, by showing it, should dishearten his army.

JOHN BATES.

He may show what outward courage he will; but I believe, as cold a night as 'tis, he could wish himself in Thames up to the neck;—and so I would he were, and I by him, at all adventures, so we were quit here.[9]

KING HENRY.

By my troth, I will speak my conscience[10] of the king: I think he would not wish himself any where but where he is.

JOHN BATES.

Then I would he were here alone; so should he be sure to be ransom'd, and a many poor men's lives saved.

KING HENRY.

I dare say you love him not so ill, to wish him here alone, howsoever you speak this, to feel other men's minds: me-

---

[1] meet: fitting. [2] element: sky; heavens. [3] shows: looks; appears. [4] conditions: qualities. [5] ceremonies: trappings. [6] stoop: swoop down (as a hawk). [7] out of doubt: undoubtedly. [8] possess . . . fear: show any sign of fear. [9] quit here: finished with this business (war). [10] my conscience: my opinion.

thinks I could not die any where so contented as in the king's company,—his cause being just, and his quarrel honourable.

MICHAEL WILLIAMS.

That's more than we know.

JOHN BATES.

Ay, or more than we should seek after; for we know enough, if we know we are the king's subjects: if his cause be wrong, our obedience to the king wipes the crime of it out of us.

MICHAEL WILLIAMS.

But if the cause be not good, the king himself hath a heavy reckoning to make, when all those legs and arms and heads, chopt off in battle, shall join together at the latter day,[1] and cry all, 'We died at such a place;' some swearing; some crying for a surgeon; some, upon their wives left poor behind them; some, upon the debts they owe; some, upon their children rawly left.[2] I am afeard there are few die well[3] that die in battle, for how can they charitably dispose of any thing, when blood is their argument? Now, if these men do not die well, it will be a black matter for the king that led them to it; who to disobey were against all proportion of subjection.[4]

KING HENRY.

So, if a son, that is by his father sent about merchandise, do sinfully miscarry upon the sea,[5] the imputation of his wickedness, by your rule, should be imposed upon his father that sent him: or if a servant, under his master's command transporting a sum of money, be assail'd by robbers, and die in many irreconciled iniquities,[6] you may call the business of the master the author of the servant's damnation:—but this is not so: the

---

[1] the latter day: the Day of Judgment.   [2] rawly left: that is, left unprovided for.   [3] die well: die a Christian death.   [4] proportion of subjection: the proper behavior of a subject to his king.   [5] do sinfully . . . sea: is lost at sea without an opportunity to confess his sins.   [6] irreconciled iniquities: unconfessed (and unforgiven) sins.

king is not bound to answer[1] the particular endings of his
soldiers, the father of his son, nor the master of his servant;
for they purpose not their death, when they purpose their
services. Besides, there is no king, be his cause never so spot-
less, if it come to the arbitrement[2] of swords, can try it out
with all unspotted soldiers: some peradventure have on them
the guilt of premeditated and contrived[3] murder; some, of be-
guiling virgins with the broken seals of perjury;[4] some, making
the wars their bulwark, that have before gored the gentle
bosom of peace with pillage and robbery. Now, if these men
have defeated the law and outrun native punishment,[5] though
they can outstrip men, they have no wings to fly from God:
war is His beadle,[6] war is His vengeance; so that here men
are punisht for before[7]-breach of the king's laws in now the
king's quarrel: where they fear'd the death, they have borne
life away; and where they would be safe, they perish: then if
they die unprovided,[8] no more is the king guilty of their
damnation, than he was before guilty of those impieties for
the which they are now visited.[9] Every subject's duty is the
king's; but every subject's soul is his own. Therefore should
every soldier in the wars do as every sick man in his bed,—
wash every mote out of his conscience: and dying so, death is
to him advantage; or not dying, the time was blessedly lost
wherein such preparation was gain'd: and in him that escapês,
it were not sin to think that, making God so free an offer,[10]
He let him outlive that day to see His greatness, and to teach
others how they should prepare.

---

[1] bound to answer: responsible for.   [2] arbitrement: decision.
[3] contrived: plotted.   [4] broken seals of perjury: false vows.
[5] native punishment: punishment in their own country.   [6] beadle:
the official who handles the arrest and sentencing of lawbreakers;
therefore, chastiser.   [7] before: previous.   [8] unprovided: i.e.,
without the last rites of the church.   [9] visited: punished.   [10] so
free an offer: such a free-will offering.

MICHAEL WILLIAMS.

'Tis certain, every man that dies ill, the ill upon his own head,
—the king is not to answer it.[1]

JOHN BATES.

I do not desire he should answer for me; and yet I determine
to fight lustily for him.

KING HENRY.

I myself heard the king say he would not be ransom'd.

MICHAEL WILLIAMS.

Ay, he said so, to make us fight cheerfully: but when our
throats are cut, he may be ransom'd, and we ne'er the wiser.

KING HENRY.

If I live to see it, I will never trust his word after.

MICHAEL WILLIAMS.

'Mass, you'll pay[2] him then! That's a perilous shot out of an
elder-gun,[3] that a poor and a private[4] displeasure can do
against a monarch! you may as well go about[5] to turn the
sun to ice with fanning in his face with a peacock's feather.
You'll never trust his word after! come, 'tis a foolish saying.

KING HENRY.

Your reproof is something too round:[6] I should be angry with
you, if the time were convenient.

MICHAEL WILLIAMS.

Let it be a quarrel between us, if you live.

KING HENRY.

I embrace it.

MICHAEL WILLIAMS.

How shall I know thee again?

KING HENRY.

Give me any gage[7] of thine, and I will wear it in my bonnet:

---

[1] answer it: answer for it.   [2] pay: punish.   [3] elder-gun: popgun
made of elder wood.   [4] a poor and a private: a poor commoner's.
[5] go about: undertake.   [6] something too round: somewhat too
plainspoken (direct).   [7] gage: token.

then, if ever thou darest acknowledge it, I will make it my quarrel.

MICHAEL WILLIAMS.

Here's my glove: give me another of thine.

KING HENRY.

There.

MICHAEL WILLIAMS.

This will I also wear in my cap: if ever thou come to me and say, after to-morrow, 'This is my glove,' by this hand, I will take thee[1] a box on the ear.

KING HENRY.

If ever I live to see it, I will challenge it.

MICHAEL WILLIAMS.

Thou darest as well be hang'd.

KING HENRY.

Well, I will do it, though I take thee in the king's company.

MICHAEL WILLIAMS.

Keep thy word: fare thee well.

JOHN BATES.

Be friends, you English fools, be friends: we have French quarrels enow,[2] if you could tell how to reckon.

KING HENRY.

Indeed, the French may lay twenty French crowns[3] to one, they will beat us; for they bear them on their shoulders: but it is no English treason to cut French crowns; and to-morrow the king himself will be a clipper.[4]   [*Exeunt* SOLDIERS.

Upon the king!—let us our lives, our souls,
Our debts, our careful[5] wives,
Our children, and our sins, lay on the king!
We must bear all. O hard condition,

---

[1] take thee: give you.   [2] enow: enough.   [3] crowns: a pun on the double meaning of the word—"coin" and "head."   [4] a clipper: a person who mutilates coins (crowns) by chipping gold from them.   [5] careful: full of care; anxious.

Twin-born with greatness, subject to the breath
Of every fool,[1] whose sense no more can feel
But his own wringing! [2]
What infinite heart's-ease must kings neglect,
That private men[3] enjoy!
And what have kings, that privates have not too,
Save ceremony,—save general ceremony?
And what art thou, thou idol ceremony?
What kind of god art thou, that suffer'st more
Of mortal griefs than do thy worshippers?
What are thy rents? what are thy comings-in? [4]
O ceremony, show me but thy worth!
What is thy soul, O adoration? [5]
Art thou aught else but place, degree, and form,
Creating awe and fear in other men?
Wherein thou art less happy being fear'd
Than they in fearing.
What drink'st thou oft, instead of homage sweet,
But poison'd flattery? O, be sick, great greatness,
And bid thy ceremony give thee cure!
Think'st thou the fiery fever will go out
With titles blown from adulation?
Will it give place to flexure[6] and low bending?
Canst thou, when thou command'st the beggar's knee,
Command the health of it? No, thou proud dream,
That play'st so subtly with a king's repose:
I am a king that find thee; and I know
'Tis not the balm,[7] the sceptre, and the ball,
The sword, the mace, the crown imperial,
The intertissued robe of gold and pearl,[8]
The farced title running 'fore the king,[9]
The throne he sits on, nor the tide of pomp

---

[1] subject . . . fool: exposed to the remarks of even the lowliest of
his subjects.   [2] whose sense . . . wringing: who is conscious only
of his own suffering.   [3] private men: commoners.   [4] comings-in:
income.   [5] What . . . adoration: what is the essential thing in
you that men adore.   [6] flexure: bowing; curtsying.   [7] balm:
anointing oil.   [8] intertissued . . . pearl: robe interwoven with
gold and pearls.   [9] The farced title . . . king: the puffed-up,
high-sounding titles preceding the name of the king, such as "His
Most Gracious Majesty," etc.

That beats upon the high shore of this world,—
No, not all these, thrice-gorgeous ceremony,
Not all these, laid in bed majestical,
Can sleep so soundly as the wretched slave,
Who, with a body fill'd and vacant mind,
Gets him to rest, cramm'd with distressful bread;[1]
Never sees horrid night, the child of hell;
But, like a lackey, from the rise to set,
Sweats in the eye of Phœbus,[2] and all night
Sleeps in Elysium;[3] next day, after dawn,
Doth rise, and help Hyperion to his horse;[4]
And follows so[5] the ever-running year,
With profitable labour, to his grave:
And, but for ceremony, such a wretch,
Winding up days with toil and nights with sleep,
Had the fore-hand[6] and vantage of a king.
The slave, a member of the country's peace,
Enjoys it; but in gross brain little wots[7]
What watch the king keeps to maintain the peace,
Whose hours the peasant best advantages.[8]

Enter ERPINGHAM.

SIR THOMAS ERPINGHAM.
My lord, your nobles, jealous of[9] your absence,
Seek through your camp to find you.

KING HENRY.

                                        Good old knight,
Collect them all together at my tent:
I'll be before thee.

SIR THOMAS ERPINGHAM.

                        I shall do't, my lord.   [*Exit.*

KING HENRY.
O God of battles! steel my soldiers' hearts;
Possess them not with fear; take from them now

---

[1] distressful bread: that is, bread earned by painful labor.
[2] Phœbus: the sun.   [3] Elysium: Paradise.   [4] help Hyperion to
his horse: that is, is up before the sun (Hyperion is another name
for the sun god).   [5] so: in this manner.   [6] fore-hand: upper
hand; advantage.   [7] wots: knows.   [8] the peasant best advantages: most benefit the peasant.   [9] jealous of: disturbed by.

The sense of reckoning, if th'opposed numbers
Pluck their hearts from them!—Not to-day, O Lord,
O, not to-day, think not upon the fault[1]
My father made in compassing[2] the crown!
I Richard's body have interred new;[3]
And on it have bestow'd more contrite tears
Than from it issued forced drops of blood:
Five hundred poor I have in yearly pay,
Who twice a-day their wither'd hands hold up
Toward heaven, to pardon blood; and I have built
Two chantries,[4] where the sad and solemn priests
Sing still[5] for Richard's soul. More will I do;
Though all that I can do is nothing worth,
Since that my penitence comes after all,
Imploring pardon.

Enter GLOSTER.

DUKE OF GLOSTER.
My liege!
    KING HENRY.
        My brother Gloster's voice?—Ay;
I know thy errand, I will go with thee:—
The day, my friends, and all things stay for me.

                                      [*Exeunt.*

Scene II.

The French camp.

Enter the DAUPHIN, ORLEANS, RAMBURES, *and others.*

DUKE OF ORLEANS.
The sun doth gild our armour; up, my lords!
    DAUPHIN.
Montez à cheval![6]—My horse! *varlet,*[7] *laquais!*[8] ha!

---

[1] fault: treason.   [2] compassing: obtaining.   [3] new: anew; Richard's body was removed from Langley to Westminster.   [4] chantries: monasteries.   [5] still: always; continuously.   [6] *Montez à cheval*: Shakespeare's French for "Mount your horse"; to horse.   [7] *varlet*: attendant; valet.   [8] *laquais*: lackey.

DUKE OF ORLEANS.

O brave spirit!

DAUPHIN.

Via!—les eaux et la terre,—[1]

DUKE OF ORLEANS.

Rien puis? l'air et le feu,—[2]

DAUPHIN.

Ciel [3] cousin Orleans.

Enter CONSTABLE.

Now, my lord Constable!

THE CONSTABLE OF FRANCE.

Hark, how our steeds for present[4] service neigh!

DAUPHIN.

Mount them, and make incision in their hides,
That their hot blood may spin in English eyes,
And dout them[5] with superfluous courage, ha!

RAMBURES.

What, will you have them weep our horses' blood?
How shall we, then, behold their natural tears?

Enter a MESSENGER.

MESSENGER.

The English are embattled,[6] you French peers.

THE CONSTABLE OF FRANCE.

To horse, you gallant princes! straight to horse!
Do but behold yond poor and starved band,
And your fair show shall suck away their souls,
Leaving them but the shales[7] and husks of men.
There is not work enough for all our hands;
Scarce blood enough in all their sickly veins
To give each naked curtle-axe[8] a stain,
That our French gallants shall to-day draw out,
And sheathe for lack of sport: let us but blow on them,

---

[1] *Via!—les eaux et la terre:* away (over) water and land.   [2] *Rien puis? l'air et le feu:* nothing more? not the air and fire, too.   [3] *Ciel:* the sky.   [4] present: immediate.   [5] dout them: put them out.   [6] embattled: in battle array.   [7] shales: shells.   [8] curtle-axe: cutlass; broadsword.

The vapour of our valour will o'erturn them.
'Tis positive 'gainst all exceptions,[1] lords,
That our superfluous lackeys and our peasants,—
Who in unnecessary action swarm
About our squares[2] of battle,—were enow
To purge this field of such a hilding[3] foe;
Though we upon this mountain's basis by
Took stand for idle speculation,—[4]
But that our honour must not. What's to say?
A very little little let us do,
And all is done. Then let the trumpets sound
The tucket-sonance[5] and the note to mount:
For our approach shall so much dare[6] the field,
That England shall couch down in fear, and yield.

Enter GRANDPRÉ.

GRANDPRÉ.

Why do you stay so long, my lords of France?
Yond island carrions, desperate of their bones,[7]
Ill-favouredly become the morning field:
Their ragged curtains[8] poorly are let loose,
And our air shakes them passing scornfully:
Big Mars[9] seems bankrout[10] in their beggar'd host,
And faintly through a rusty beaver[11] peeps:
The horsemen sit like fixed candlesticks,
With torch-staves in their hand; and their poor jades
Lob down[12] their heads, dropping the hides and hips,
The gum down-roping from their pale-dead eyes,
And in their pale dull mouths the gimmal-bit[13]
Lies foul with chew'd grass, still and motionless;
And their executors, the knavish crows,
Fly o'er them, all impatient for their hour.

---

[1] 'Tis positive . . . exceptions: there's no doubt about it.
[2] squares: squadrons.   [3] hilding: menial; worthless.   [4] for idle speculation: as onlookers; idle spectators.   [5] tucket-sonance: trumpet call to the cavalry.   [6] dare: dazzle.   [7] desperate . . . bones: i.e., without hope of saving their bones.   [8] curtains: banners.   [9] Mars: god of war.   [10] bankrout: bankrupt.   [11] beaver: helmet visor.   [12] Lob down: droop.   [13] gimmalbit: a bit made of links.

Description cannot suit itself[1] in words
To demonstrate the life of such a battle
In life so lifeless as it shows itself.

THE CONSTABLE OF FRANCE.

They have said their prayers, and they stay for death.

DAUPHIN.

Shall we go send them dinners and fresh suits,
And give their fasting horses provender,
And after fight with them?

THE CONSTABLE OF FRANCE.

I stay but for my guidon:[2]—to the field!—
I will the banner from a trumpet take,
And use it for[3] my haste. Come, come, away!
The sun is high, and we outwear[4] the day.   [*Exeunt.*

SCENE III.

The English camp.

Enter GLOSTER, BEDFORD, EXETER, ERPINGHAM, *with all his host;* SALISBURY, *and* WESTMORELAND.

DUKE OF GLOSTER.

Where is the king?

DUKE OF BEDFORD.

The king himself is rode[5] to view the battle.

EARL OF WESTMORELAND.

Of fighting-men they have full three-score thousand.

DUKE OF EXETER.

There's five to one; besides, they all are fresh.

EARL OF SALISBURY.

God's arm strike with us! 'tis a fearful odds.

---

[1] suit itself: clothe itself.
[2] guidon: standard; banner.
[3] for: because of.
[4] outwear: are wasting.
[5] is rode: has ridden.

God b' wi' you, princes all; I'll to my charge:[1]
If we no more meet till we meet in heaven,
Then, joyfully,—my noble Lord of Bedford,—
My dear Lord Gloster,—and my good Lord Exeter,—
And my kind kinsman,[2]—warriors all, adieu!

    DUKE OF BEDFORD.

Farewell, good Salisbury; and good luck go with thee!

    DUKE OF EXETER.

Farewell, kind lord; fight valiantly to-day:
And yet I do thee wrong to mind[3] thee of it,
For thou art framed[4] of the firm truth of valour.

                        [*Exit* SALISBURY.

    DUKE OF BEDFORD.

He is as full of valour as of kindness;
Princely in both.

Enter KING HENRY.

    EARL OF WESTMORELAND.

           O, that we now had here
But one ten thousand of those men in England
That do no work to-day!

    KING HENRY.

               What's he that wishes so?
My cousin Westmoreland?—No, my fair cousin:
If we are markt to die, we are enow[5]
To do our country loss; and if to live,
The fewer men, the greater share of honour.
God's will! I pray thee, wish not one man more.
By Jove, I am not covetous for gold;
Nor care I who doth feed upon[6] my cost;
It yearns[7] me not if men my garments wear;

---

[1] charge: battle station.   [2] kinsman: Westmoreland.   [3] mind: remind.   [4] framed: built.   [5] enow: enough.   [6] upon: at.
[7] yearns: grieves.

Such outward things dwell not in my desires:
But if it be a sin to covet honour,
I am the most offending soul alive.
No, faith, my coz,[1] wish not a man from England:
God's peace! I would not lose so great an honour,
As one man more, methinks, would share from me,
For the best hope I have. O, do not wish one more!
Rather proclaim it, Westmoreland, through my host,
That he which hath no stomach to this fight,
Let him depart; his passport shall be made,
And crowns for convoy[2] put into his purse:
We would not die in that man's company
That fears his fellowship to die with us.[3]
This day is call'd the feast of Crispian:[4]
He that outlives this day, and comes safe home,
Will stand a tip-toe when this day is named,
And rouse him at the name of Crispian.
He that shall live[5] this day, and see old age,
Will yearly on the vigil feast his neighbours,
And say, 'To-morrow is Saint Crispian:'
Then will he strip his sleeve and show his scars,
And say, 'These wounds I had on Crispin's day.'
Old men forget; yet all shall be forgot,
But he'll remember with advantages[6]
What feats he did that day: then shall our names,
Familiar in their mouths as household words,—
Harry the king, Bedford and Exeter,
Warwick and Talbot, Salisbury and Gloster,—
Be in their flowing cups freshly remember'd.
This story shall the good man teach his son;

---

[1] coz: cousin (used of almost any degree of kinship).   [2] convoy:
traveling expenses.   [3] That fears . . . us: who fears to be my
companion in death.   [4] the feast of Crispian: October 25; Crispin
and Crispinian were Roman brothers who went to France to advance Christianity and were beheaded by Maximianus about 287;
they are the patron saints of shoemakers.   [5] live: survives.
[6] with advantages: that is, with additions and elaborations.

And Crispin Crispian shall ne'er go by,
From this day to the ending of the world,
But we in it shall be remembered,—
We few, we happy few, we band of brothers;
For he to-day that sheds his blood with me
Shall be my brother; be he ne'er so vile,[1]
This day shall gentle his condition:[2]
And gentlemen in England now a-bed
Shall think themselves accurst they were not here;
And hold their manhoods cheap whiles any speaks
That fought with us upon Saint Crispin's day.

Enter SALISBURY.

EARL OF SALISBURY.

My sovereign lord, bestow yourself[3] with speed:
The French are bravely[4] in their battles set,
And will with all expedience[5] charge on us.

KING HENRY.

All things are ready, if our minds be so.

EARL OF WESTMORELAND.

Perish the man whose mind is backward now!

KING HENRY.

Thou dost not wish more help from England, coz?

EARL OF WESTMORELAND.

God's will! my liege, would you and I alone,
Without more help, might fight this battle out!

KING HENRY.

Why, now thou hast unwisht five thousand men;
Which likes me better[6] than to wish us one.—
You know your places: God be with you all!

Tucket. Enter MONTJOY.

MONTJOY.

Once more I come to know of thee, King Harry,
If for thy ransom thou wilt now compound,[7]

---

[1] so vile: of such humble birth.   [2] gentle his condition: "advance
him to the rank of gentleman"—Johnson.   [3] bestow yourself: repair to your posts.   [4] bravely: in gallant array.   [5] expedience:
haste.   [6] likes me better: pleases me more.   [7] compound: reach
agreement.

Before thy most assured overthrow:
For certainly thou art so near the gulf,[1]
Thou needs must be englutted.[2] Besides, in mercy,
The Constable desires thee thou wilt mind[3]
Thy followers of repentance; that their souls
May make a peaceful and a sweet retire[4]
From off these fields, where, wretches, their poor bodies
Must lie and fester.

    KING HENRY.

                Who hath sent thee now?

    MONTJOY.

The Constable of France.

    KING HENRY.

I pray thee, bear my former answer back:
Bid them achieve[5] me, and then sell my bones.
Good God! why should they mock poor fellows thus?
The man that once did sell the lion's skin
While the beast lived, was kill'd with[6] hunting him.
A many of our bodies shall no doubt
Find native[7] graves; upon the which, I trust,
Shall witness live in brass of this day's work:
And those that leave their valiant bones in France,
Dying like men, though buried in your dunghills,
They shall be famed; for there the sun shall greet them,
And draw their honours reeking up to heaven;
Leaving their earthly parts to choke your clime,
The smell whereof shall breed a plague in France.

---

[1] gulf: whirlpool.   [2] englutted: swallowed up.   [3] mind: remind.
[4] retire: retreat.   [5] achieve: conquer; kill.   [6] with: while.   [7] native: English.

Mark, then, abounding[1] valour in our English;
That, being dead, like to the bullet's grazing,
Break out into a second course of mischief,
Killing in relapse of mortality.[2]
Let me speak proudly:[3]—tell the Constable
We are but warriors for the working-day;[4]
Our gayness and our gilt are all besmircht
With rainy marching in the painful field;
There's not a piece of feather in our host,—
Good argument, I hope, we will not fly,—
And time hath worn us into slovenry:[5]
But, by the mass, our hearts are in the trim;[6]
And my poor soldiers tell me, yet ere night
They'll be in fresher robes; or they will pluck[7]
The gay new coats o'er the French soldier's heads,
And turn them out of service. If they do this,—
As, if God please, they shall,—my ransom then
Will soon be levied. Herald, save thou thy labour;
Come thou no more for ransom, gentle herald:
They shall have none, I swear, but these my joints,—
Which if they have as I will leave 'em them,
Shall yield them little, tell the Constable.

　　　MONTJOY.
I shall, King Harry. And so, fare thee well:
Thou never shalt hear herald any more.　　　　　　　[*Exit.*
　　　KING HENRY.
I fear thou'lt once more come again for ransom.

　　　　　　　　　Enter YORK.

　　　DUKE OF YORK.
My lord, most humbly on my knee I beg
The leading of the vaward.[8]

---

[1] abounding: abundant.　[2] relapse of mortality: "a rebound of
death in deadliness"—Schmidt.　[3] Let me speak proudly: that is,
let me forget my jesting.　[4] for the working-day: in our working
clothes; not in the splendid trappings of soldiers, and not here on
holiday.　[5] slovenry: slovenliness.　[6] in the trim: in fine dress or
condition.　[7] or they will pluck: though they have to pluck.
[8] vaward: vanguard.

KING HENRY.

Take it, brave York.[1]—Now, soldiers, march away:—
And how thou pleasest, God, dispose the day!   [*Exeunt.*

SCENE IV.

The field of battle.

Alarum: excursions. Enter PISTOL, *French* SOLDIER, *and* BOY.

PISTOL.

Yield, cur!

FRENCH SOLDIER.

Je pense que vous êtes le gentilhomme de bonne qualité.[2]

PISTOL.

Qualtitie calmie custure me! [3] Art thou a gentleman? what is
thy name? discuss.

FRENCH SOLDIER.

O Seigneur Dieu! [4]

PISTOL.

O, Signieur Dew should be a gentleman:—
Perpend[5] my words, O Signieur Dew, and mark;—
O Signieur Dew, thou diest on point of fox,[6]
Except, O signieur, thou do give to me
Egregious[7] ransom.

FRENCH SOLDIER.

O, prenez miséricorde! ayez pitié de moy! [8]

PISTOL.

Moy shall not serve; I will have forty moys;
Or I will fetch thy rim[9] out at thy throat

---

[1] York: Edward, Duke of York.   [2] *Je pense . . . qualité:* I believe that you are a gentleman.   [3] *calmie custure me:* Johnson
interprets this phrase as Pistol's quotation from a contemporary
Irish song—"callino, castore me."   [4] *Seigneur Dieu:* Lord God;
but Pistol takes this for the soldier's name.   [5] Perpend: consider;
weigh.   [6] fox: a common word for sword; the figure of a fox
was engraved on a certain kind of sword as the trade-mark.
[7] Egregious: extraordinarily high.   [8] *moy:* Pistol thinks that *moy*
(*moi*) is a coin.   [9] thy rim: the lining of your stomach.

In drops of crimson blood.

FRENCH SOLDIER.

Est-il impossible d'échapper la force de ton bras? [1]

PISTOL.

Brass, cur!
Thou damned and luxurious[2] mountain-goat,
Offer'st me brass?

FRENCH SOLDIER.

O, pardonnez-moy!

PISTOL.

Say'st thou me so? is that a ton of moys?—
Come hither, boy: ask me this slave in French
What is his name.

BOY.

Écoutez: comment êtes-vous appelé?

FRENCH SOLDIER.

Monsieur le Fer.

BOY.

He says his name is Master Fer.

PISTOL.

Master Fer! I'll fer him, and firk[3] him, and ferret[4] him:—
discuss the same in French unto him.

BOY.

I do not know the French for fer, and ferret, and firk.

PISTOL.

Bid him prepare; for I will cut his throat.

FRENCH SOLDIER.

Que dit-il, monsieur?

BOY.

*Il me commande de vous dire que vous faites vous prêt; car
ce soldat ici est disposé tout à cette heure de couper votre
gorge.* [5]

---

[1] *Est-il . . . bras:* is it impossible to escape the force of his arm.
[2] luxurious: lustful.
[3] firk: beat.
[4] ferret: worry (as a ferret worries a rat before killing it).
[5] *Il . . . gorge:* he commands me to tell you that you should protect
yourself, for this soldier is disposed at this time to cut your throat.

PISTOL.

Owy, cuppele gorge, permafoy,[1]

Peasant, unless[2] thou give me crowns, brave crowns;
Or mangled shalt thou be by this my sword.

FRENCH SOLDIER.

*O, je vous supplie, pour l'amour de Dieu, me pardonner! Je
suis gentilhomme de bonne maison: gardez ma vie, et je vous
donnerai deux cents écus.*

PISTOL.

What are his words?

BOY.

He prays you to save his life: he is a gentleman of a good
house; and for his ransom he will give you two hundred
crowns.

PISTOL.

Tell him my fury shall abate, and I
The crowns will take.

FRENCH SOLDIER.

Petit monsieur, que dit-il? [3]

BOY.

*Encore qu'il est contre son jurement de pardonner aucun
prisonnier, néanmoins, pour les écus que vous l'avez promis,
il est content de vous donner la liberté, le franchisement.*[4]

FRENCH SOLDIER.

*Sur mes genoux je vous donne mille remercîmens; et je
m'estime heureux que je suis tombé entre les mains d'un
chevalier, je pense, le plus brave, vaillant, et très distingué
seigneur d'Angleterre.*[5]

PISTOL.

Expound unto me,[6] boy.

---

[1] *Owy, cuppele gorge, permafoy:* Pistol's version of "oh, yes, cut
the throat, on my honor."   [2] unless: either.   [3] *que dit-il:* what
did he say.   [4] *Encore . . . franchisement:* he says it is against
his judgment to pardon any prisoner; nevertheless, for the crowns
you promise, he is willing to give you your liberty.   [5] *Sur . . .
d'Angleterre:* the boy's translation is given on the next page.
[6] Expound unto me: explain to me.

BOY.

He gives you, upon his knees, a thousand thanks; and he es-
teems himself happy that he hath faln into the hands of one,
as he thinks, the most brave, valorous, and thrice-worthy
signieur of England.

PISTOL.

As I suck blood, I will some mercy show.—Follow me, cur.
[*Exit.*

BOY.

Suivez-vous le grand capitaine.[1] [*Exit* FRENCH SOLDIER.] I
did never know so full a voice issue from so empty a heart:
but the saying is true,—The empty vessel makes the greatest
sound. Bardolph and Nym had ten times more valour than
this roaring devil i'th'old play,[2] that every one may pare his
nails with a wooden dagger; and they are both hang'd; and
so would this be, if he durst steal any thing adventurously.[3]
I must stay with the lackeys, with the luggage of our camp:
the French might have a good prey of us, if he knew of
it; for there is none to guard it but boys.   [*Exit.*

SCENE V.

Another part of the field.

Enter CONSTABLE, ORLEANS, BOURBON, DAUPHIN, RAMBURES,
and others.

THE CONSTABLE OF FRANCE.

O diable!

DUKE OF ORLEANS.

O Seigneur!—le jour est perdu, tout est perdu! [4]

DAUPHIN.

Mort de ma vie! all is confounded,[5] all!

---

[1] *Suivez-vous le grand capitaine:* follow the great captain.
[2] roaring devil i'th'old play: in the old miracle plays, the devil
usually entered roaring and carrying a wooden dagger or sword.
[3] adventurously: boldly.
[4] *le jour est perdu . . . perdu:* the day is lost; all is lost.
[5] confounded: ruined; lost.

Reproach and everlasting shame
Sit mocking in our plumes.—*O méchante fortune!*—[1]
Do not run away.   [*A short alarum.*

THE CONSTABLE OF FRANCE.
                    Why, all our ranks are broke.

DAUPHIN.
O perdurable[2] shame!—let's stab ourselves.
Be these the wretches that we play'd at dice for?

DUKE OF ORLEANS.
Is this the king we sent to for his ransom?

DUKE OF BOURBON.
Shame, and eternal shame, nothing but shame!
Let's die in honour: once more back again;
And he that will not follow Bourbon now,
Let him go hence, and with his cap in hand,
Like a base pandar,[3] hold the chamber-door
Whilst by a slave, no gentler[4] than my dog,
His fairest daughter is contaminate.

THE CONSTABLE OF FRANCE.
Disorder, that hath spoil'd us, friend[5] us now!
Let us on heaps[6] go offer up our lives.

DUKE OF ORLEANS.
We are enow, yet living in the field,
To smother up the English in our throngs,
If any order might be thought upon.

DUKE OF BOURBON.
The devil take order now! I'll to the throng:
Let life be short; else shame will be too long.   [*Exeunt.*

---

[1] *méchante fortune:* evil fortune.
[2] perdurable: lasting; enduring.
[3] pandar: pander; procurer.
[4] gentler: better born.
[5] friend: befriend.
[6] on heaps: in a body.

Scene VI.

Another part of the field.

Alarum. Enter KING HENRY *and* FORCES, EXETER, *and others.*

KING HENRY.

Well have we done, thrice-valiant countrymen:
But all's not done; yet keep the French the field.

DUKE OF EXETER.

The Duke of York commends him to your majesty.

KING HENRY.

Lives he, good uncle? thrice within this hour
I saw him down; thrice up again, and fighting;
From helmet to the spur all blood[1] he was.

DUKE OF EXETER.

In which array, brave soldier, doth he lie,
Larding[2] the plain; and by his bloody side,
Yoke-fellow to his honour-owing[3] wounds,
The noble Earl of Suffolk also lies.
Suffolk first died: and York, all haggled over,[4]
Comes to him, where in gore he lay insteept,[5]
And takes him by the beard; kisses the gashes
That bloodily did yawn upon his face;
And cries aloud, 'Tarry, dear cousin Suffolk!
My soul shall thine keep company to heaven;
Tarry, sweet soul, for mine, then fly abreast;
As in this glorious and well-foughten field
We kept together in our chivalry!'
Upon these words I came, and cheer'd him up:
He smiled me in the face,[6] raught me his hand,[7]
And, with a feeble gripe,[8] says, 'Dear my lord,
Commend my service to my sovereign.'
So did he turn, and over Suffolk's neck

---

[1] all blood: covered with blood.   [2] Larding: enriching.
[3] honour-owing: honorable.   [4] all haggled over: cut or hacked
over his entire body.   [5] insteept: soaked.   [6] smiled me in the
face: smiled into my face.   [7] raught me his hand: reached for my
hand.   [8] gripe: grip.

He threw his wounded arm, and kist his lips;
And so, espoused[1] to death, with blood he seal'd
A testament[2] of noble-ending love.
The pretty[3] and sweet manner of it forced
Those waters[4] from me which I would have stopt;
But I had not so much of man in me,
And all my mother[5] came into mine eyes,
And gave me up to tears.

    KING HENRY.

               I blame you not;
For, hearing this, I must perforce compound
With[6] mistful eyes, or they will issue too.—   [*Alarum.*
But, hark! what new alarum is this same?—
The French have reinforced their scatter'd men:—
Then every soldier kill his prisoners;
Give the word through.   [*Exeunt.*

SCENE VII.

Another part of the field.

Enter FLUELLEN *and* GOWER.

    FLUELLEN.

Kill the poys and the luggage! [7] 'tis expressly against the law
of arms: 'tis as arrant[8] a piece of knavery, mark you now,
as can be offert; in your conscience, now, is it not?

    GOWER.

'Tis certain there's not a boy left alive; and the cowardly
rascals that ran from the battle ha' done this slaughter: besides, they have burn'd and carried away all that was in the

---

[1] espoused: wedded.   [2] testament: last will and testament.
[3] pretty: lovely.   [4] waters: tears.   [5] all my mother: all the fem-
inine softness in me.   [6] compound/With: come to terms with.
[7] Kill . . . luggage: the English equipment was guarded by boys
and lackeys, who were set upon by some of the French soldiers and
killed, the *luggage* plundered.   [8] arrant: out-and-out.

king's tent; wherefore the king, most worthily, hath caused
every soldier to cut his prisoner's throat. O, 'tis a gallant king!

FLUELLEN.

Ay, he was porn at Monmouth, Captain Gower. What call
you the town's name where Alexander the Pig was porn?

GOWER.

Alexander the Great.

FLUELLEN.

Why, I pray you, is not pig great? the pig, or the great, or
the mighty, or the huge, or the magnanimous, are all one
reckonings, save the phrase is a little variations.

GOWER.

I think Alexander the Great was born in Macedon: his father
was call'd Philip of Macedon, as I take it.

FLUELLEN.

I think it is in Macedon where Alexander is porn. I tell you,
captain, if you look in the maps of the 'orld, I warrant you
sall[1] find, in the comparisons between Macedon and Monmouth, that the situations, look you, is both alike. There is
a river in Macedon; and there is also moreover a river at
Monmouth: it is called Wye at Monmouth; but it is out of
my prains[2] what is the name of the other river; but 'tis all
one,[3] 'tis alike as my fingers is to my fingers, and there is
salmons in both. If you mark Alexander's life well, Harry of
Monmouth's life is come after it indifferent[4] well; for there is
figures[5] in all things. Alexander,—Got knows, and you know,

---

[1] sall: shall.
[2] it is out of my prains: I have forgotten.
[3] all one: all the same; no matter.
[4] indifferent: equally.
[5] figures: parallels; prototypes.

—in his rages, and his furies, and his wraths, and his cholers,[1]
and his moods, and his displeasures, and his indignations,
and also being a little intoxicates in his prains, did, in his
ales and his angers, look you, kill his pest friend, Cleitus.

GOWER.

Our king is not like him in that: he never kill'd any of his
friends.

FLUELLEN.

It is not well done, mark you now, to take the tales out of
my mouth, ere it is made and finisht. I speak but in the figures and comparisons of it: as Alexander kill'd his friend
Cleitus, being in his ales and his cups; so also Harry Monmouth, being in his right wits and his goot judgements,
turn'd away the fat knight with the great-pelly doublet:[2]
he was full of jests, and gipes,[3] and knaveries, and mocks;
I have forgot his name.

GOWER.

Sir John Falstaff.

FLUELLEN.

That is he:—I'll tell you there is goot men porn at Monmouth.

GOWER.

Here comes his majesty.

Alarum. Enter KING HENRY *and* FORCES; WARWICK, GLOSTER,
EXETER, *and others.*

KING HENRY.

I was not angry since I came to France
Until this instant.—Take a trumpet, herald;
Ride thou unto the horsemen on yond hill:
If they will fight with us, bid them come down,

---

[1] cholers: ill humors.
[2] the fat knight . . . doublet: Falstaff.
[3] gipes: gibes.

Or void[1] the field; they do offend our sight:
If they'll do neither, we will come to them,
And make them skirr[2] away, as swift as stones
Enforced from the old Assyrian slings:
Besides, we'll cut the throats of those we have;
And not a man of them that we shall take
Shall taste our mercy:—go, and tell them so.

DUKE OF EXETER.

Here comes the herald of the French, my liege.

DUKE OF GLOSTER.

His eyes are humbler than they used to be.

Enter MONTJOY.

KING HENRY.

How now! what means this, herald? know'st thou not
That I have fined these bones of mine for ransom? [3]
Comest thou again for ransom?

MONTJOY.

                              No, great king:
I come to thee for charitable licence
That we may wander o'er this bloody field
To look[4] our dead, and then to bury them;
To sort our nobles from our common men;
For many of our princes—woe the while—
Lie drown'd and soakt in mercenary blood;[5]
So do our vulgar drench their peasant limbs
In blood of princes; and their wounded steeds
Fret fetlock[6] deep in gore, and with wild rage
Yerk out[7] their armed[8] heels at their dead masters,
Killing them twice. O, give us leave, great king,
To view the field in safety, and dispose
Of their dead bodies!

---

[1] void: leave.   [2] skirr: scurry.   [3] fined . . . ransom: that is, the king has won the battle and his bones, which he wagered as ransom, remain his own.   [4] look: seek out.   [5] mercenary blood: the blood of common soldiers who fought for money.   [6] Fret fetlock: gnaw at their fetlocks.   [7] Yerk out: lash out.   [8] armed: spiked.

KING HENRY.

                    I tell thee truly, herald,
I know not if the day be ours or no;
For yet a many of your horsemen peer[1]
And gallop o'er the field.

MONTJOY.

                         The day is yours.

KING HENRY.

Praised be God, and not our strength, for it!—
What is this castle call'd that stands hard by?[2]

MONTJOY.

They call it Agincourt.

KING HENRY.

Then call we this the field of Agincourt,
Fought on the day of Crispin Crispianus.[3]

FLUELLEN.

Your grandfather[4] of famous memory, an't please your majesty, and your great-uncle Edward the Plack Prince of Wales, as I have read in the chronicles, fought a most prave pattle here in France.

KING HENRY.

They did, Fluellen.

FLUELLEN.

Your majesty says very true: if your majesties is remember'd of it, the Welshmen did goot service in a garden where leeks[5] did grow, wearing leeks in their Monmouth caps; which, your majesty knows, to this hour in an honourable padge of the service; and I do pelieve your majesty takes no scorn to wear the leek upon Saint Tavy's day.[6]

KING HENRY.

I wear it for a memorable honour;
For I am Welsh, you know, good countryman.

---

[1] peer: appear.
[2] hard by: nearby.
[3] the day of Crispin Crispianus: the Feast of Crispin and Crispinian.
[4] grandfather: Henry's great-grandfather, Edward III.
[5] leeks: the floral symbol of Wales.
[6] Saint Tavy's day: St. David's Day—see Act IV, sc. i, p. 89.

FLUELLEN.

All the water in Wye cannot wash your majesty's Welsh
plood out of your pody, I can tell you that: Got pless it, and
preserve it, as long as it pleases his grace, and his majesty too!

KING HENRY.

Thanks, good my countryman.

FLUELLEN.

By Cheshu, I am your majesty's countryman, I care not who
know it; I will confess it to all the 'orld: I need not to be
ashamed of your majesty, praised be Got, so long as your
majesty is an honest[1] man.

KING HENRY.

God keep me so!—Our heralds go with him:
Bring me just notice[2] of the numbers dead
On both our parts.—Call yonder fellow hither.

    [*Points to* WILLIAMS. *Exeunt* HERALDS *with* MONTJOY.

DUKE OF EXETER.

Soldier, you must come to the king.

KING HENRY.

Soldier, why wear'st thou that glove in thy cap?

MICHAEL WILLIAMS.

An't please your majesty, 'tis the gage of one that I should
fight withal, if he be alive.

KING HENRY.

An Englishman?

MICHAEL WILLIAMS.

An't please your majesty, a rascal that swagger'd with me[3]
last night; who, if alive, and ever dare to challenge this glove,
I have sworn to take him a box o'th'ear: or if I can see my

---

[1] honest: honorable.
[2] just notice: exact information.
[3] swagger'd with me: bullied me; bandied words with me.

glove in his cap, which he swore, as he was a soldier, he
would wear if alive, I will strike it out soundly.

KING HENRY.

What think you, Captain Fluellen? is it fit this soldier keep
his oath?

FLUELLEN.

He is a craven and a villain else, an't please your majesty,
in my conscience.

KING HENRY.

It may be his enemy is a gentleman of great sort,[1] quite from
the answer of his degree.[2]

FLUELLEN.

Though he be as goot a gentleman as the tevil is,[3] as Lucifer
and Belzebub himself, it is necessary, look your Grace, that
he keep his vow and his oath: if he be perjured,[4] see you
now, his reputation is as arrant a villain and a Jack-sauce,[5]
as ever his plack shoe trod upon Got's ground and his earth,
in my conscience, la.

KING HENRY.

Then keep thy vow, sirrah, when thou meet'st the fellow.

MICHAEL WILLIAMS.

So I will, my liege, as I live.

KING HENRY.

Who servest thou under?

MICHAEL WILLIAMS.

Under Captain Gower, my liege.

FLUELLEN.

Gower is a goot captain, and is goot knowledge and litera-
tured in the wars.

KING HENRY.

Call him hither to me, soldier.

---

[1] of great sort: of high rank.   [2] from the answer . . . degree:
that is, debarred by the laws of duello from answering a challenge
from a person of lower rank.   [3] as goot (good) a gentleman as
the tevil (devil) is: a proverbial expression.   [4] perjured: forsworn.
[5] Jack-sauce: Saucy Jack; impudent fellow: Jack is often used by
Shakespeare as a term of contempt.

MICHAEL WILLIAMS.

I will, my liege.   [*Exit.*

KING HENRY.

Here, Fluellen; wear thou this favour for me, and stick it in
thy cap: when Alençon[1] and myself were down together, I
pluckt this glove from his helm: if any man challenge this,
he is a friend to Alençon, and an enemy to our person; if
thou encounter any such, apprehend him, and thou dost me
love.

FLUELLEN.

Your Grace does me as great honours as can be desired in
the hearts of his subjects: I would fain see the man, that
has but two legs, that shall find himself aggriefed at this
glove; that is all; but I would fain see it once, an please Got
of his grace that I might see.

KING HENRY.

Know'st thou Gower?

FLUELLEN.

He is my dear friend, an please you.

KING HENRY.

Pray thee, go seek him, and bring him to my tent.

FLUELLEN.

I will fetch him.

KING HENRY.

My Lord of Warwick, and my brother Gloster,
Follow Fluellen closely at the heels:
The glove which I have given him for a favour
May haply[2] purchase him[3] a box o'th'ear;
It is the soldier's; I, by bargain, should
Wear it myself. Follow, good cousin Warwick:
If that the soldier strike him,—as I judge

---

[1] Alençon: John, the first Duke of Alençon, bested by King Henry
and killed by the king's men at the Battle of Agincourt, according
to Holinshed.

[2] haply: perhaps.

[3] purchase him: get himself.

By his blunt bearing, he will keep his word,—
Some sudden mischief may arise of it;
For I do know Fluellen valiant,
And, toucht with choler,[1] hot as gunpowder,
And quickly will return an injury:
Follow, and see there be no harm between them.—
Go you with me, uncle of Exeter.   [*Exeunt.*

SCENE VIII.

Before KING HENRY'S *pavilion.*

Enter GOWER *and* WILLIAMS.

MICHAEL WILLIAMS.
I warrant it is to knight you, captain.

Enter FLUELLEN.

FLUELLEN.
Got's will and his pleasure, captain, I peseech you now, come apace[2] to the king: there is more goot toward you peradventure than is in your knowledge to dream of.

MICHAEL WILLIAMS.
Sir, know you this glove?

FLUELLEN.
Know the glove! I know the glove is a glove.

MICHAEL WILLIAMS.
I know this; and thus I challenge it.   [*Strikes him.*

FLUELLEN.
'Splood,[3] an arrant traitor as any's in the universal 'orld, or in France, or in England!

GOWER.
How now, sir! you villain!

MICHAEL WILLIAMS.
Do you think I'll be forsworn? [4]

---

[1] choler: quickness of temper.
[2] apace: quickly.
[3] 'Splood: God's blood (a mild oath).
[4] be forsworn: break my oath.

FLUELLEN.

Stand away, Captain Gower; I will give treason his payment into plows, I warrant you.

MICHAEL WILLIAMS.

I am no traitor.

FLUELLEN.

That's a lie in thy throat.—[1] I charge you in his majesty's name, apprehend him: he's a friend of the Duke Alençon's.

Enter WARWICK *and* GLOSTER.

EARL OF WARWICK.

How now, how now! what's the matter?

FLUELLEN.

My Lord of Warwick, here is—praised be Got for it!—a most contagious[2] treason come to light, look you, as you shall desire in a summer's day.—Here is his majesty.

Enter KING HENRY *and* EXETER.

KING HENRY.

How now! what's the matter?

FLUELLEN.

My liege, here is a villain and a traitor, that, look your Grace, has struck the glove which your majesty is take out of the helmet of Alençon.

MICHAEL WILLIAMS.

My liege, this was my glove; here is the fellow of it; and he that I gave it to in change[3] promised to wear it in his cap: I promised to strike him, if he did: I met this man with my glove in his cap, and I have been as good as my word.

FLUELLEN.

Your majesty hear now, saving your majesty's manhood,[4] what an arrant, rascally, beggarly, lousy knave it is: I hope

---

[1] lie . . . throat: an insult demanding payment by mortal combat.

[2] contagious: pestilential.

[3] in change: in exchange.

[4] saving your majesty's manhood: an apology for Fluellen's plain-spokenness.

your majesty is pear me testimony, and witness, and will avouchment,[1] that this is the glove of Alençon, that your majesty is give me, in your conscience, now.

KING HENRY.

Give me thy glove, soldier: look, here is the fellow of it.
'Twas I, indeed, thou promised'st to strike;
And thou hast given me most bitter terms.[2]

FLUELLEN.

An please your majesty, let his neck answer for it, if there is any martial law in the 'orld.

KING HENRY.

How canst thou make me satisfaction?

MICHAEL WILLIAMS.

All offences, my liege, come from the heart: never came any from mine that might offend your majesty.

KING HENRY.

It was ourself thou didst abuse.

MICHAEL WILLIAMS.

Your majesty came not like yourself: you appear'd to me but as a common man; witness the night, your garments, your lowliness;[3] and what your highness suffer'd under that shape, I beseech you take it for your own fault, and not mine: for had you been as I took you for, I made no offence; therefore, I beseech your highness, pardon me.

KING HENRY.

Here, uncle Exeter, fill this glove with crowns,
And give it to this fellow.—Keep it, fellow;
And wear it for an honour in thy cap

---

[1] avouchment: affirm.
[2] bitter terms: bitter words; insults.
[3] lowliness: humble bearing.

Till I do challenge it.—Give him the crowns:—
And, captain, you must needs be friends with him.

FLUELLEN.

By this day and this light, the fellow has mettle enough in his pelly.—Hold, there is twelve pence for you; and I pray you to serve Got, and keep you out of prawls, and prabbles,[1] and quarrels, and dissensions, and, I warrant you, it is the petter for you.

MICHAEL WILLIAMS.

I will none of your money.

FLUELLEN.

It is with a goot will; I can tell you, it will serve you to mend your shoes: come, wherefore should you be so pashful? Your shoes is not so goot: 'tis a goot[2] silling, I warrant you, or I will change it.

Enter an English HERALD.

KING HENRY.

Now, herald,—are the dead number'd?[3]

HERALD.

Here is the number of the slaughter'd French.

[Delivers a paper.

KING HENRY.

What prisoners of good sort[4] are taken, uncle?

DUKE OF EXETER.

Charles duke of Orleans, nephew to the king;
John duke of Bourbon, and Lord Bouciqualt:
Of other lords and barons, knights and squires,
Full fifteen hundred, besides common men.

KING HENRY.

This note doth tell me of ten thousand French
That in the field lie slain: of princes, in this number,

---

[1] **prabbles:** squabbles; quarrels.
[2] **goot:** good; not counterfeit.
[3] **number'd:** counted.
[4] **good sort:** high rank.

And nobles bearing banners,[1] there lie dead
One hundred twenty-six: added to these,
Of knights, esquires, and gallant gentlemen,
Eight thousand and four hundred; of the which,
Five hundred were but yesterday dubb'd knights:[2]
So that, in these ten thousand they have lost,
There are but sixteen hundred mercenaries;[3]
The rest are princes, barons, lords, knights, squires,
And gentlemen of blood and quality.
The names of those their nobles that lie dead,—
Charles Delabreth, high-Constable of France;
Jaques of Chatillon, admiral of France;
The master of the cross-bows, Lord Rambures;
Great-master of France, the brave Sir Guiscard Dauphin;
John duke of Alençon; Antony duke of Brabant,
The brother to the Duke of Burgundy;
And Edward duke of Bar: of lusty earls,
Grandpré and Roussi, Fauconberg and Foix,
Beaumont and Marle, Vaudemont and Lestrale.
Here was a royal fellowship of death!—
Where is the number of our English dead?—

                 [HERALD *presents another paper.*

Edward the duke of York, the Earl of Suffolk,
Sir Richard Ketly, Davy Gam, esquire;
None else of name; and of all other men
But five and twenty.—O God, Thy arm was here;
And not to us, but to Thy arm alone,
Ascribe we all!—When, without stratagem,
But in plain shock and even play of battle,
Was ever known so great and little loss
On one part and on th'other?—Take it, God,

---

[1] **bearing banners**: bearing banners or standards on which their coats-of-arms were emblazoned.
[2] **were but yesterday dubb'd knights**: that is, were only yesterday made knights by the king, in a ceremony in which he tapped the knight on the shoulder with his sword and said, "I dub thee knight."
[3] **mercenaries**: hired or paid soldiers.

For it is only Thine!

DUKE OF EXETER.

'Tis wonderful!

KING HENRY.

Come, go we in procession to the village:
And be it death proclaimed through our host
To boast of this, or take that praise from God
Which is His only.

FLUELLEN.

Is it not lawful, an please your majesty, to tell how many is
kill'd?

KING HENRY.

Yes, captain; but with this acknowledgement,
That God fought for us.

FLUELLEN.

Yes, my conscience, He did us great goot.

KING HENRY.

Do we all holy rites:
Let there be sung *Non nobis* and *Te Deum*.
The dead with charity enclosed in clay,
We'll then to Calais; and to England then;
Where ne'er from France arrived more happy men.

[*Exeunt.*

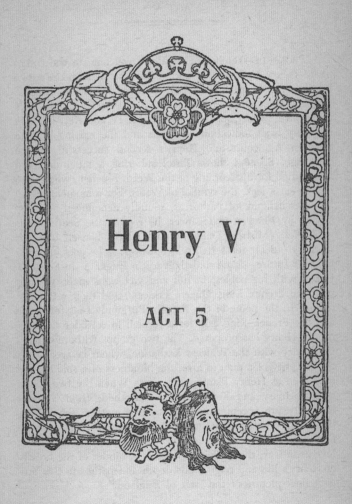

Henry V

ACT 5

ACT V

THE PROLOGUE sketches in London's welcome to the triumphant Henry V, hopefully anticipating in Shakespeare's own
time such a return for the Earl of Essex, who is in Ireland,
quelling a rebellion in the name of Queen Elizabeth. Five
years have, in fact, passed between Act IV and Act V. There
is a very brief indication of events and the passing of time
between Agincourt and Henry's second successful French
campaign. Scene i shows Pistol suffering a much-deserved
humiliation for his scorning of the Welsh Fluellen, who forces
him to eat a leek, the symbol of Wales. For a moment, Pistol
becomes a figure of pathos as, soundly denounced and dis-
missed by Fluellen and Gower, he reports the death of his
wife, Nell (Mistress Quickly), and admits himself old. His
rascality quickly reasserts itself, however, as he goes off plan-
ning his future—fraud and thievery in England. In Scene ii,
Henry with his nobles, in full and victorious majesty, meet
with the French King, Queen, Princess, and their retinue of
nobles. In the name of the French, Burgundy sues for peace
and the French King asks for a council to consider the conditions Henry has proposed. The two groups withdraw, leaving Henry with the Princess Katharine, whom he woos with
the sincerity of a man in love, the bluntness of a soldier, and
only then as Henry Plantagenet, King. When the two courts
return, Henry and Katharine are betrothed; Henry's terms
for peace are accepted and Katharine's mother, the Queen,
blesses the coming marriage. The play's culmination lies in the
final, irresistible figure of Henry V, human and triumphant in
love as in war; the Epilogue, with its reminder of the brevity
of Henry's life and reign, adds depth and pathos to this bril-
liant final picture of the "star of England."

ACT V.   PROLOGUE.

Enter CHORUS.

CHORUS.
Vouchsafe to those that have not read the story,
That I may prompt them: and of such as have,
I humbly pray them to admit th'excuse

Of time, of numbers, and due course of things,
Which cannot in their huge and proper life
Be here presented. Now we bear the king
Towards Calais: grant him there; there seen,
Heave him away upon your winged thoughts
Athwart the sea. Behold, the English beach
Pales in[1] the flood with men, with wives, and boys,
Whose shouts and claps out-voice the deep-mouth'd sea,
Which, like a mighty whiffler[2] 'fore the king,
Seems to prepare his way: so let him land;
And solemnly[3] see him set on to London.
So swift a pace hath thought, that even now
You may imagine him upon Blackheath;
Where that his lords desire him to have borne
His bruised helmet and his bended sword
Before him through the city: he forbids it,
Being free from vainness and self-glorious pride;
Giving full trophy, signal, and ostent,
Quite from himself to God.[4] But now behold,
In the quick forge and working-house[5] of thought,
How London doth pour out her citizens!
The mayor, and all his brethren, in best sort,—[6]
Like to the senators of th'antique Rome,
With the plebeians swarming at their heels,—
Go forth, and fetch their conquering Cæsar in:
As, by a lower but loving likelihood,[7]
Were now the general[8] of our gracious empress—
As in good time he may—from Ireland coming,
Bringing rebellion broached[9] on his sword,
How many would the peaceful city quit,
To welcome him! much more, and much more cause,

---

[1] Pales in: encircles; fences in.   [2] whiffler: an official who walks first in royal processions, to clear the way.   [3] solemnly: ceremoniously.   [4] Giving full trophy . . . God: "Transferring all the honours of conquest, all tokens, trophies, and shows, from himself to God"—Johnson.   [5] working-house: workshop.   [6] in best sort: in their best manners and clothes.   [7] but loving likelihood: but also eagerly anticipated probability.   [8] the general: the Earl of Essex.   [9] broached: spitted.

Did they this Harry. Now in London place him;—
As yet the lamentation of the French
Invites the King of England's stay at home;—
The emperor[1] coming in behalf of France,
To order peace between them;—and omit
All the occurrences, whatever chanced,
Till Harry's back-return again[2] to France:
There must we bring him; and myself have play'd
The interim, by remembering[3] you 'tis past.
Then brook abridgement;[4] and your eyes advance,
After your thoughts, straight back again to France.

[Exit.

Scene I.

France. The English camp.

Enter FLUELLEN and GOWER.

GOWER.

Nay, that's right; but why wear you your leek to-day? Saint
Davy's day is past.

FLUELLEN.

There is occasions and causes why and wherefore in all things:
I will tell you, asse my friend, Captain Gower:—the rascally,
scald,[5] peggarly, lousy, pragging knave, Pistol,—which you
and yourself, and all the 'orld, know to be no petter than a
fellow, look you now, of no merits,—he is come to me, and
prings me pread and salt yesterday, look you, and pid me eat
my leek: it was in a place where I could not preed no con-
tention with him; but I will be so pold as to wear it in my cap
till I see him once again, and then I will tell him a little piece
of my desires.

---

[1] The emperor: the German emperor Sigismund, who was married
to Henry's second cousin, visited London on May 1, 1416, to try to
negotiate between Henry and the French king.   [2] Harry's back-
return again: the king goes back again.   [3] remembering: re-
minding.   [4] brook abridgement: that is, endure or bear with us in
this omission.   [5] scald: scurvy; scaly.

GOWER.

Why, here he comes, swelling like a turkeycock.

FLUELLEN.

'Tis no matter for his swellings nor his turkeycocks.

Enter PISTOL.

Got pless you, Auncient Pistol! you scurvy, lousy knave, Got pless you!

PISTOL.

Ha! art thou bedlam? [1] dost thou thirst, base Trojan,
To have me fold up Parca's fatal web? [2]
Hence! I am qualmish[3] at the smell of leek.

FLUELLEN.

I peseech you heartily, scurvy, lousy knave, at my desires, and my requests, and my petitions, to eat, look you, this leek: because, look you, you do not love it, nor your affections, and your appetites, and your disgestions, does not agree with it, I would desire you to eat it.

PISTOL.

Not for Cadwallader and all his goats.[4]

FLUELLEN.

There is one goat for you. [*Strikes him.*] Will you be so goot, scald knave, as eat it?

PISTOL.

Base Trojan,[5] thou shalt die.

FLUELLEN.

You say very true, scald knave,—when Got's will is: I will desire you to live in the mean time, and eat your victuals: come, there is sauce for it. [*Strikes him again.*] You call'd me yesterday mountain-squire;[6] but I will make you to-day a

---

[1] bedlam: lunatic; mad; a corruption for Bethlehem, a London hospital for the insane.   [2] fold up Parca's fatal web: the Parcae (the Fates) had control over human life; therefore, cut the thread of life.   [3] qualmish: squeamish.   [4] Cadwallader and all his goats: Cadwallader was the last of the Welsh kings, and goats are plentiful in Wales.   [5] Trojan: a common term of opprobrium.   [6] mountain-squire: a man with worthless land; hence, a poor man.

squire of low degree. I pray you, fall to: if you can mock a
leek, you can eat a leek.

GOWER.

Enough, captain: you have astonisht[1] him.

FLUELLEN.

I say, I will make him eat some part of my leek, or I will peat
his pate four days.—Pite, I pray you; it is goot for your green[2]
wound and your ploody coxcomb.[3]

PISTOL.

Must I bite?

FLUELLEN.

Yes, certainly, and out of doubt,[4] and out of question too, and
ambiguities.

PISTOL.

By this leek, I will most horribly revenge:
I eat and eat, I swear—

FLUELLEN.

Eat, I pray you: will you have some more sauce to your
leek? there is not enough leek to swear by.

PISTOL.

Quiet thy cudgel; thou dost see I eat.

FLUELLEN.

Much goot do you, scald knave, heartily. Nay, pray you,
throw none away; the skin is goot for your proken coxcomb.
When you take occasions to see leeks hereafter, I pray you,
mock at 'em; that is all.

PISTOL.

Good.

FLUELLEN.

Ay leeks is goot:—hold you, there is a groat[5] to heal your
pate.

---

[1] astonisht: stunned.
[2] green: fresh; raw.
[3] coxcomb: head.
[4] out of doubt: without doubt.
[5] groat: English fourpence.

PISTOL.

Me a groat!

FLUELLEN.

Yes, verily and in truth, you shall take it; or I have another leek in my pocket, which you shall eat.

PISTOL.

I take thy groat in earnest of revenge.[1]

FLUELLEN.

If I owe you any thing, I will pay you in cudgels; you shall be a woodmonger,[2] and buy nothing of me but cudgels. Got b' wi' you, and keep you. and heal your pate.   [*Exit.*

PISTOL.

All hell shall stir for this.

GOWER.

Go, go; you are a counterfeit cowardly knave. Will you mock at an ancient tradition,—begun upon an honourable respect,[3] and worn as a memorable trophy of predeceased valour,—and dare not avouch in your deeds any of your words? I have seen you gleeking and galling[4] at this gentleman twice or thrice. You thought, because he could not speak English in the native garb,[5] he could not therefore handle an English cudgel: you find it otherwise; and henceforth let a Welsh correction teach you a good English condition.[6] Fare ye well.

[*Exit.*

PISTOL.

Doth Fortune play the huswife[7] with me now?
News have I, that my Nell is dead i'th'spital [8]
Of malady of France;[9]

---

[1] in earnest of revenge: i.e., in token (part payment) of the revenge you owe me.   [2] woodmonger: seller of wood.   [3] upon an honourable. respect: for an honorable reason.   [4] gleeking and galling: sneering and scoffing.   [5] garb: fashion.   [6] condition: disposition.   [7] huswife: housewife; hussy.   [8] spital: hospital.   [9] malady of France: venereal disease.

And there my rendezvous is quite cut off.
Old I do wax;[1] and from my weary limbs
Honour is cudgell'd. Well, bawd[2] will I turn,
And something[3] lean to cutpurse of quick hand.
To England will I steal, and there I'll steal:
And patches will I get unto these scars,
And swear I got them in the Gallia[4] wars.   [*Exit.*

Scene II.

France. The French KING'S palace.

Enter, at one door, KING HENRY, BEDFORD, GLOSTER, EXETER,
WARWICK, WESTMORELAND, *and other* LORDS; *at another, the
French* KING, QUEEN ISABEL, *the* PRINCESS KATHARINE, ALICE,
other LADIES, *and* LORDS; *the* DUKE OF BURGUNDY, *and his*
TRAIN.

KING HENRY.
Peace to this meeting, wherefore[5] we are met!
Unto our brother France, and to our sister,
Health and fair time of day;—joy and good wishes
To our most fair and princely cousin Katharine;—
And as a branch and member of this royalty,
By whom this great assembly is contrived,
We do salute you, Duke of Burgundy;—
And, princes French, and peers, health to you all!
FRENCH KING.
Right joyous are we to behold your face,
Most worthy brother England; fairly met:—
So are you, princes English, every one.
QUEEN ISABEL.
So happy be the issue, brother England,
Of this good day and of this gracious meeting,

---

[1] wax: grow.
[2] bawd: procurer; keeper of a brothel.
[3] something: somewhat.
[4] Gallia: French.
[5] wherefore: for which.

As we are now glad to behold your eyes;
Yours eyes, which hitherto have borne in them
Against the French, that met them in their bent,
The fatal balls of murdering basilisks:[1]
The venom of such looks, we fairly hope,
Have lost their quality; and that this day
Shall change all griefs and quarrels into love.

KING HENRY.

To cry amen to that, thus we appear.

QUEEN ISABEL.

You English princes all, I do salute you.

DUKE OF BURGUNDY.

My duty to you both, on equal love,[2]
Great Kings of France and England! That I have labour'd,
With all my wits, my pains, and strong endeavours,
To bring your most imperial majesties
Unto this bar[3] and royal interview,
Your mightiness on both parts best can witness.
Since, then, my office hath so far prevail'd,
That, face to face and royal eye to eye,
You have congreeted,[4] let it not disgrace me,
If I demand, before this royal view,
What rub[5] or what impediment there is,
Why that the naked, poor, and mangled Peace,
Dear nurse of arts, plenties, and joyful births,
Should not, in this best garden of the world,
Our fertile France, put up her lovely visage?
Alas, she hath from France too long been chased!
And all her husbandry doth lie on heaps,
Corrupting in its own fertility.
Her vine,[6] the merry cheerer of the heart,

---

[1] The fatal balls . . . basilisks: the eyes of the fabled basilisk were said to kill at a glance; with a pun on the double meaning of cannonballs.   [2] on equal love: springing from equal love for both of you.   [3] bar: court.   [4] congreeted: greeted each other.   [5] rub: hindrance.   [6] vine: grapevines.

Unpruned dies; her hedges even-pleacht,[1]
Like prisoners wildly overgrown with hair,
Put forth disorder'd twigs; her fallow leas[2]
the darnel,[3] hemlock, and rank fumitory,[4]
Do root upon, while that the coulter[5] rusts,
That should deracinate[6] such savagery;
The even mead, that erst[7] brought sweetly forth
The freckled cowslip, burnet, and green clover,
Wanting[8] the scythe, all uncorrected, rank,
Conceives by idleness,[9] and nothing teems
But hateful docks, rough thistles, kecksies,[10] burs,
Losing both beauty and utility.
And as our vineyards, fallows, meads, and hedges,
Defective in their natures, grow to wildness,
Even so our houses, and ourselves and children,
Have lost, or do not learn for want of time,
The sciences that should become our country;
But grow, like savages,—as soldiers will,
That nothing do but meditate on blood,—
To swearing, and stern looks, diffused[11] attire,
And every thing that seems unnatural.
Which to reduce into our former favour,
You are assembled: and my speech entreats
That I may know the let,[12] why gentle Peace
Should not expel these inconveniences,
And bless us with her former qualities.

  KING HENRY.

If, Duke of Burgundy, you would the peace,
Whose want gives growth to th'imperfections
Which you have cited, you must buy that peace
With full accord to all our just demands;
Whose tenours[13] and particular effects
You have, enscheduled[14] briefly, in your hands.

---

[1] even-pleacht: with the branches smoothly intertwined.   [2] fallow leas: meadows lying fallow (untilled).   [3] darnel: a weed that grows in plowed fields.   [4] rank fumitory: luxuriant fumaria.   [5] coulter: plow blade.   [6] deracinate: uproot.   [7] erst: formerly.   [8] Wanting: lacking.   [9] Conceives by idleness: idleness fathers the weeds.   [10] kecksies: dried stalks.   [11] diffused: disordered.   [12] let: hindrance.   [13] tenours: substance.   [14] enscheduled: listed.

DUKE OF BURGUNDY.

The king hath heard them; to the which as yet
There is no answer made.

KING HENRY.

Well, then, the peace,
Which you before so urged, lies in his answer.

FRENCH KING.

I have but with a cursorary[1] eye
O'erglanced[2] the articles: pleaseth your Grace
To appoint some of your council presently[3]
To sit with us once more, with better heed
To re-survey them, we will suddenly
Pass our accept and peremptory answer.[4]

KING HENRY.

Brother, we shall.—Go, uncle Exeter,—
And brother Clarence,—and you, brother Gloster,—
Warwick,—and Huntingdon,—go with the king;
And take with you free power to ratify,
Augment, or alter, as your wisdoms best
Shall see advantageable[5] for our dignity,
Any thing in or out of our demands;
And we'll consign[6] thereto.—Will you, fair sister,
Go with the princes, or stay here with us?

QUEEN ISABEL.

Our gracious brother, I will go with them:
Haply[7] a woman's voice may do some good,
When articles too nicely urged[8] be stood on.[9]

KING HENRY.

Yet leave our cousin Katharine here with us:
She is our capital demand, comprised
Within the fore-rank of our articles.

QUEEN ISABEL.

She hath good leave.

---

[1] cursorary: cursory; hasty. [2] O'erglanced: glanced over.
[3] presently: immediately. [4] Pass . . . answer: give the answer
on which we finally agree. [5] advantageable: advantageous.
[6] consign: agree. [7] Haply: happily; perhaps. [8] too nicely
urged: in too much detail, or with too much concern over trifles.
[9] stood on: insisted upon.

[Exeunt all except KING HENRY, KATHARINE, *and* ALICE.

KING HENRY.

Fair Katharine, and most fair!
Will you vouchsafe to teach a soldier terms
Such as will enter at a lady's ear,
And plead his love-suit to her gentle heart?

KATHARINE.

Your majesty shall mock at me; I cannot speak your England.

KING HENRY.

O fair Katharine, if you will love me soundly with your French heart, I will be glad to hear you confess it brokenly with your English tongue. Do you like me, Kate?

KATHARINE.

Pardonnez-moi, I cannot tell vat is 'like me.'

KING HENRY.

An angel is like you, Kate, and you are like an angel.

KATHARINE.

Que dit-il? que je suis semblable à les anges?[1]

ALICE.

Oui, vraiment, sauf votre grace, ainsi dit-il.

KING HENRY.

I said so, dear Katharine; and I must not blush to affirm it.

KATHARINE.

O bon Dieu! les langues des hommes sont pleines de tromperies.

KING HENRY.

What says she, fair one? that the tongues of men are full of deceits?

---

[1] *Que dit-il? que je suis semblable à les anges?*: what did he say? that I am like the angels?

ALICE.

Oui, dat de tongues of de mans is be full of deceits—dat is de princess.[1]

KING HENRY.

The princess is the better Englishwoman.[2] I'faith, Kate, my wooing is fit for thy understanding: I am glad thou canst speak no better English; for, if thou couldst, thou wouldst find me such a plain king, that thou wouldst think I had sold my farm to buy my crown. I know no ways to mince it[3] in love, but directly to say, 'I love you:' then, if you urge me further than to say, 'Do you in faith?' I wear out my suit.[4] Give me your answer; i'faith, do; and so clap hands[5] and a bargain: how say you, lady?

KATHARINE.

Sauf votre honneur, me understand vell.

KING HENRY.

Marry, if you would put me to verses or to dance for your sake, Kate, why, you undid me:[6] for the one, I have neither words nor measure;[7] and for the other, I have no strength in measure, yet a reasonable measure in strength. If I could win a lady at leap-frog, or by vaulting into my saddle with my armour on my back, under the correction of[8] bragging be it spoken, I should quickly leap into a wife. Or if I might buffet[9] for my love, or bound my horse for her favours, I could lay on like a butcher, and sit like a jack-an-apes,[10] never off. But, before God, Kate, I cannot look greenly,[11] nor gasp out my eloquence, nor I have no cunning in protestation; only downright oaths, which I never use till urged, nor never break for

---

[1] dat is de princess: that is what the princess says.　[2] The princess . . . Englishwoman: that is, Katharine recognizes his flattery for what it is.　[3] mince it: speak in a fancy fashion.　[4] wear . . . suit: have nothing further to say.　[5] clap hands: clasp hands.　[6] you undid me: you would put me to shame.　[7] measure: dancing, with a pun on *meter* and *amount*.　[8] under . . . correction of: with apologies for.　[9] buffet: box.　[10] jack-an-apes: a pet monkey.　[11] look greenly: act like a lovesick youth.

urging. If thou canst love a fellow of this temper, Kate, whose
face is not worth sun-burning,[1] that never looks in his glass
for love of any thing he sees there,—let thine eye be thy
cook.[2] I speak to thee plain soldier: if thou canst love me for
this, take me; if not, to say to thee that I shall die, is true,—
but for thy love, by the Lord, no; yet I love thee too. And
while thou livest, dear Kate, take a fellow of plain and uncoin'd constancy;[3] for he perforce must do thee right, because
he hath not the gift to woo in other places: for these fellows
of infinite tongue, that can rime themselves into ladies' favours,
they do always reason themselves out again. What! a speaker
is but a prater; a rime is but a ballad. A good leg will fall; a
straight back will stoop; a black beard will turn white; a
curl'd pate will grow bald; a fair face will wither; a full eye
will wax hollow: but a good heart, Kate, is the sun and the
moon; or, rather, the sun, and not the moon,—for it shines
bright, and never changes, but keeps his course truly. If thou
would have such a one, take me: and take me, take a soldier;
take a soldier, take a king: and what say'st thou, then, to my
love? speak, my fair, and fairly, I pray thee.

KATHARINE.

Is it possible dat I sould love de enemy of France?

KING HENRY.

No; it is not possible you should love the enemy of France,
Kate: but, in loving me, you should love the friend of France;
for I love France so well, that I will not part with a village of
it; I will have it all mine: and, Kate, when France is mine and

---

[1] not worth sun-burning: i.e., so ugly that the sun cannot hurt it.
[2] be thy cook: dress the dish (me) to suit yourself.
[3] uncoin'd constancy: genuine faithfulness.

I am yours, then yours is France and you are mine.

KATHARINE.

I cannot tell vat is dat.

KING HENRY.

No, Kate? I will tell thee in French; which I am sure will hang upon my tongue like a new-married wife about her husband's neck, hardly to be shook off. *Je quand sur le possession de France, et quand vous avez le possession de moi,—* let me see, what then? Saint Denis[1] be my speed!—*donc votre est France et vous êtes mienne.* It is as easy for me, Kate, to conquer the kingdom, as to speak so much more French: I shall never move thee in French, unless it be to laugh at me.

KATHARINE.

Sauf votre honneur, le Français que vous parlez, il est meilleur que l'Anglais lequel je parle.

KING HENRY.

No, faith, is't not, Kate: but thy speaking of my tongue, and I thine, most truly-falsely, must needs be granted to be much at one.[2] But, Kate, dost thou understand thus much English,— Canst thou love me?

KATHARINE.

I cannot tell.

KING HENRY.

Can any of your neighbours tell, Kate? I'll ask them. Come, I know thou lovest me: and at night, when you come into your closet,[3] you'll question this gentlewoman about me; and I know, Kate, you will to her dispraise those parts in me that you love with your heart: but, good Kate, mock me merci-

---

[1] Saint Denis: the patron saint of France.
[2] at one: alike.
[3] your closet: your bedchamber.

fully; the rather, gentle princess, because I love thee cruelly.
If ever thou beest mine, Kate,—as I have a saving faith within
me tells me thou shalt,—I get thee with scambling,[1] and thou
must therefore needs prove a good soldier-breeder: shall not
thou and I, between Saint Denis and Saint George, compound
a boy, half French, half English, that shall go to Constanti-
nople and take the Turk by the beard? shall we not? what
say'st thou, my fair flower-de-luce? [2]

KATHARINE.

I do not know dat.

KING HENRY.

No; 'tis hereafter to know, but now to promise: do but now
promise, Kate, you will endeavour for your French part of
such a boy; and for my English moiety[3] take the word of a
king and a bachelor. How answer you, *la plus belle Katharine
du monde, mon très-chère et devin déesse?* [4]

KATHARINE.

Your majestee ave *fausse*[5] French enough to deceive de most
sage demoiselle dat is *en France.*

KING HENRY.

Now, fie upon my false French! By mine honour, in true
English, I love thee, Kate: by which honour I dare not swear
thou lovest me; yet my blood begins to flatter me that thou
dost, notwithstanding the poor and untempering[6] effect of
my visage. Now, beshrew[7] my father's ambition! he was thinking of civil wars when he got[8] me: therefore was I created
with a stubborn[9] outside, with an aspect of iron, that, when I
come to woo ladies, I fright them. But, in faith, Kate, the elder
I wax, the better I shall appear: my comfort is, that old age,

---

[1] scambling: scrambling; struggling (in the war).   [2] flower-de-
luce: fleur-de-lis, the royal emblem of France; the iris.   [3] moiety:
share; half.   [4] *la plus . . . déesse:* the most beautiful girl in the
world, and my very dear and divine goddess.   [5] *fausse:* false.
[6] untempering: incapable of being softened.   [7] beshrew: a mild
curse.   [8] got: begot.   [9] stubborn: rough.

that ill layer-up[1] of beauty, can do no more spoil upon my
face: thou hast me, if thou hast me, at the worst; and thou
shalt wear me, if thou wear me, better and better:—and therefore tell me, most fair Katharine, will you have me? Put off
your maiden blushes; avouch the thoughts of your heart with
the looks of an empress; take me by the hand, and say, 'Harry
of England, I am thine:' which word thou shalt no sooner bless
mine ear withal, but I will tell thee aloud, 'England is thine,
Ireland is thine, France is thine, and Henry Plantagenet is
thine;' who, though I speak it before his face, if he be not
fellow with the best king, thou shalt find the best king of good
fellows. Come, your answer in broken music,—[2] for thy voice
is music, and thy English broken; therefore, queen of all
Katharines, break thy mind to me in broken English,—wilt
thou have me?

KATHARINE.

Dat is as it sall[3] please de *roi mon père*.[4]

KING HENRY.

Nay, it will please him well, Kate,—it shall please him, Kate.

KATHARINE.

Den it sall also content me.

KING HENRY.

Upon that I kiss your hand, and I call you my queen.

KATHARINE.

*Laissez, mon seigneur, laissez, laissez: ma foi, je ne veux point
que vous abaissiez votre grandeur en baisant la main d'une*

---

[1] layer-up: preserver.
[2] broken music: music arranged in parts (here used as a pun).
[3] sall: shall.
[4] de *roi mon pére*: the king, my father.

*votre indigne serviteur; excusez-moi, je vous supplie, mon très-
puissant seigneur.*[1]

KING HENRY.

Then I will kiss your lips, Kate.

KATHARINE.

*Les dames et demoiselles pour être baisées devant leur noces,
il n'est pas la coutume de France.*

KING HENRY.

Madam my interpreter, what says she?

ALICE.

Dat it is not de fashion *pour les* ladies of France,—I cannot
tell vat is *baiser en Anglish.*

KING HENRY.

To kiss.

ALICE.

Your majestee *entendre* bettre *que moi.*

KING HENRY.

It is not a fashion for the maids in France to kiss before they
are married, would she say?

ALICE.

Oui, vraiment.

KING HENRY.

O Kate, nice[2] customs court'sy[3] to great kings. Dear Kate, you
and I cannot be confined within the weak list[4] of a country's
fashion: we are the makers of manners, Kate; and the liberty
that follows our places[5] stops the mouth of all find-faults,[6]—
as I will do yours for upholding the nice fashion of your
country in denying me a kiss: therefore, patiently and yield-
ing. [*Kissing her.*] You have witchcraft in your lips, Kate:
there is more eloquence in a sugar touch of them than in the

---

[1] *Laissez . . . seigneur:* let go, my lord, let go, let go. My faith, I
do not wish that you should abuse your greatness in kissing the hand
of one of your Lordship's unworthy servants. Excuse me, I beg of
you, my very powerful lord.   [2] nice: punctilious.   [3] court'sy:
bow.   [4] weak list: frail or slight boundary.   [5] follows our places:
goes along with our rank.   [6] find-faults: faultfinders.

tongues of the French council; and they should sooner per-
suade Harry of England than a general petition of monarchs.
—Here comes your father.

Enter the French KING *and* QUEEN, BURGUNDY, BEDFORD, GLOS-
TER, EXETER, WESTMORELAND, WARWICK, &c.

DUKE OF BURGUNDY.

God save your majesty! my royal cousin,
Teach you our princess English?

KING HENRY.

I would have her learn, my fair cousin, how perfectly I love
her; and that is good English.

DUKE OF BURGUNDY.

Is she not apt?

KING HENRY.

Our tongue is rough, coz, and my condition[1] is not smooth;[2]
so that, having neither the voice nor the heart of flattery
about me, I cannot so conjure up the spirit of love in her,
that he will appear in his true likeness.

DUKE OF BURGUNDY.

Pardon the frankness of my mirth, if I answer you for that.
If you would conjure in her, you must make a circle; if conjure up love in her in his true likeness, he must appear naked
and blind.[3] Can you blame her, then, being a maid yet
rosed-over with the virgin crimson of modesty, if she deny
the appearance of a naked blind boy in her naked seeing self?
It were, my lord, a hard condition for a maid to consign[4] to.

KING HENRY.

Yet they do wink[5] and yield,—as love is blind[6] and enforces.

---

[1] condition: disposition.   [2] smooth: gentle.   [3] naked and blind:
Cupid, the god of Love, is always pictured as naked and sightless.
[4] consign: agree.   [5] wink: shut their eyes.   [6] blind: uncontroll-
able.

DUKE OF BURGUNDY.

They are then excused, my lord, when they see not what they do.

KING HENRY.

Then, good my lord, teach your cousin to consent winking.

DUKE OF BURGUNDY.

I will wink on her to consent, my lord, if you will teach her to know my meaning: for maids, well summer'd and warm kept, are like flies at Bartholomew-tide,[1] blind, though they have their eyes; and then they will endure handling, which before would not abide looking on.

KING HENRY.

This moral ties me over to time and a hot summer; and so I shall catch the fly, your cousin, in the latter end, and she must be blind too.

DUKE OF BURGUNDY.

As love is, my lord, before it loves.

KING HENRY.

It is so: and you may, some of you, thank love for my blindness, who cannot see many a fair French city for one fair French maid that stands in my way.

FRENCH KING.

Yes, my lord, you see them perspectively,[2] the cities turn'd into a maid; for they are all girdled with maiden walls that war hath never enter'd.

KING HENRY.

Shall Kate be my wife?

FRENCH KING.

So please you.

---

[1] Bartholomew-tide: August 24, St. Bartholomew's Day, when the evenings begin to grow chilly and flies sluggish.
[2] perspectively: a "perspective" glass presented a distortion of reality.

KING HENRY.

I am content; so the maiden cities you talk of may wait on
her:[1] so the maid that stood in the way for my wish shall
show me the way to my will.

FRENCH KING.

We have consented to all terms of reason.

KING HENRY.

Is't so, my lords of England?

EARL OF WESTMORELAND.

The king hath granted every article:—
His daughter first; and then, in sequel, all,
According to their firm proposed natures.[2]

DUKE OF EXETER.

Only, he hath not yet subscribed[3] this:
Where your majesty demands, that the King of France, having
any occasion to write for matter of grant, shall name your
highness in this form and with this addition, in French, *Notre
très-cher fils Henri, roi d'Angleterre, héritier de France;* and
thus in Latin, *Præclarissimus filius noster Henricus, rex
Angliæ, et hæres Franciæ.*[4]

FRENCH KING.

Nor this I have not, brother, so denied,
But your request shall make me let it pass.

KING HENRY.

I pray you, then, in love and dear alliance,
Let that one article rank with the rest;
And thereupon give me your daughter.

FRENCH KING.

Take her, fair son; and from her blood raise up
Issue to me; that the contending kingdoms
Of France and England, whose very shores look pale

---

[1] so the maiden cities . . . her: provided that she bring the cities
with her (as a dowry).   [2] their firm proposed natures: i.e., in the
exact form in which they were proposed.   [3] subscribed: thor-
oughly agreed to.   [4] *Præclarissimus filius noster Henricus, rex
Angliæ, et hæres Franciæ:* correctly, *praecarissimus;* proclaim you
our son Henry, King of England, and heir to the throne of France.

With envy of each other's happiness,
May cease their hatred; and this dear conjunction[1]
Plant neighbourhood and Christian-like accord
In their sweet bosoms, that never war advance
His bleeding sword 'twixt England and fair France.

ALL.

Amen!

KING HENRY.

Now, welcome, Kate;—and bear me witness all,
That here I kiss her as my sovereign queen.   [*Flourish.*

QUEEN ISABEL.

God, the best maker of all marriages,
Combine your hearts in one, your realms in one!
As man and wife, being two, are one in love,
So be there 'twixt your kingdoms such a spousal,[2]
That never may ill office, or fell[3] jealousy,
Which troubles oft the bed of blessed marriage,
Thrust in between the paction[4] of these kingdoms,
To make divorce of their incorporate league;
That English may as French, French Englishmen,
Receive each other!—God speak this Amen!

ALL.

Amen!

KING HENRY.

Prepare we for our marriage:—on which day,
My lord of Burgundy, we'll take your oath,
And all the peers', for surety[5] of our leagues.
Then shall I swear to Kate, and you to me;
And may our oaths well kept and prosperous be!

[*Sennet. Exeunt.*

---

[1] dear conjunction: solemn and important union.
[2] spousal: espousal; marriage.
[3] fell: cruel.
[4] paction: agreement; alliance.
[5] for surety: for guarantee.

Epilogue.

Enter CHORUS.

CHORUS.

Thus far, with rough and all unable[1] pen,
 Our bending[2] author hath pursued the story;
In little room confining mighty men,
 Mangling by starts[3] the full course of their glory.
Small time,[4] but in that small, most greatly liv'd
 This star of England: fortune made his sword;
By which the world's best garden[5] he achieved,
 And of it left his son imperial lord.
Henry the Sixth, in infant bands[6] crown'd king
 Of France and England, did this king succeed;
Whose state so many had the managing,
 That they lost France, and made his England bleed:
Which oft our stage hath shown;[7] and for their sake,
 In your fair minds let this acceptance take.[8]   [*Exit.*

---

[1] all unable: impotent. [2] bending: bowing; humble. [3] by
starts: by fits and starts; by a piecemeal presentation. [4] Small
time: Henry died at the age of thirty-five. [5] the world's best garden: i.e., France. [6] infant bands: swaddling clothes. [7] Which
oft . . . shown: the three parts of *Henry VI* had already become
very popular on the stage. [8] let this acceptance take: allow this
play to meet with a gracious reception.

THE AIRMONT SHAKESPEARE LIBRARY

All titles available at 50¢ each